T0152956

Creative Dressage Schooling

Enjoy the Training Process with 55 Meaningful Exercises

Translated by Lilliana Joseph

TRAFALGAR SQUARE
North Pomfret, Vermont

First published in 2014 by
Trafalgar Square Books
North Pomfret, Vermont 05053

First paperback edition 2017

Printed in the United States of America

Originally published in the German language as *Gegogene Linien und Seit-engänge* by Müller Rüschlikon Verlag, Stuttgart

Copyright © 2010 Müller Rüschlikon Verlag, Postfach 103743, 70032 Stuttgart, in cooperation with Paul Pietsch Publishing Company GmbH & Co., license holder of Bucheli Publishers
English translation © 2014 Trafalgar Square Books

All rights reserved. No part of this book may be reproduced, by any means, without written permission of the publisher, except by a reviewer quoting brief excerpts for a review in a magazine, newspaper, or website.

ISBN: 978-1-57076-860-6

Library of Congress Control Number: 2014939627

Disclaimer of Liability
The author and publisher shall have neither liability nor responsibility to any person or entity with respect to any loss or damage caused or alleged to be caused directly or indirectly by the information contained in this book. While the book is as accurate as the author can make it, there may be errors, omissions, and inaccuracies.

Trafalgar Square Books encourages the use of approved safety helmets in all equestrian sports and activities.

All photographs by Daniela Derler
Graphics by Alexandra Hawich and Martin Kuchler

Interior design by Anita Ament
Cover design by RM Didier
Typefaces: Frutiger, PT Serif

10 9 8 7 6 5 4 3 2 1

Contents

Contents

Preface: How This Book Came to Be

As a child I was ambitious and wanted to advance quickly in riding. I was lucky enough to have a highly trained and experienced dressage horse, "Ata," at my disposal. I read every piece of dressage literature that I could find (which, 20 years ago was not nearly as much as is available today!) but due to my lack of experience, I didn't fully understand what I was reading at the time. When trying to perform advanced dressage movements with Ata, my riding wasn't always completely correct. I realized this in hindsight after acquiring my first young horse, who was less forgiving of rider error than Ata had been.

Over time, as I gained maturity, I became aware of the complex knowledge called upon when riding and training horses that can only be developed with experience. The old saying, "Riding can only be learned by riding," couldn't be more true.

So it is with humility that I say that now, as a more experienced and educated rider, I am often surprised by how many amateur riders who have (understandably) caught the "horse bug," but who have no idea how to organize and ride meaningful dressage work. It doesn't matter if they are young or old, or whether they occasionally ride dressage in between trail rides or are serious about lower-level competition—there still should be a point to their schooling and variety and interest to keep their horse engaged.

Although simple gymnasticizing work isn't necessarily what we think of when we think of "dressage," it should be a consistent part of the work we do with our horses to make sure they are fit and able to carry us without incurring injury or damage. As riders we should take on this responsibility to our horses, don't you think? In addition, if—like I did—you keep analyzing your riding, you will eventually become aware of some of your riding mistakes and weaknesses, and you will want to correct them. But how?

These are things addressed in this book. I go back and discuss the basics, then suggest exercises that may seem simple to you but can be adjusted in their degree of difficulty and combined in an endless number of creative ways. You will be guided from riding simple correct corners through other bending lines, with some leg-yielding thrown in, until soon you will have arrived at half-passes.

Don't be afraid to try new things with your horse. New exercises bring a nice change of routine for both of you, and it is rewarding when they help you improve over time. Movements that were once challenging for your horse will become easier for him to perform, and he will become more supple and more fun to ride.

Have fun reading and riding!

Julia Kohl

The Right Path: The Training Scale

A correct position is a prerequisite for effective administration of the aids.

Time and experience have established a unique guideline for riders; one that is accessible to all equestrians, wherever they live and ride. This system is known as the Classical Training Scale. Unfortunately, despite considerable proliferation of the Training Scale ideals, they are still studied and followed by too few because, despite constant revisions, they seem (to some riders) "stuffy" or outdated.

Even though an understanding of the Training Scale is now expected—even required—by many dressage and riding associations, sadly, the elements are often simply memorized and repeated, when they should instead be carefully followed and considered a lifelong guide for success as a rider and trainer of horses. Actual understanding and application of the components of the Training Scale leads to harmony between rider and horse.

Riders at the beginning of their dressage "journey" may find it difficult to visualize the more advanced points of the Training Scale. Not to worry, this understanding is developed over time and by immersing yourself in the material. The more the concepts of the Training Scale are internalized and the more you follow the Training Scale while practicing dressage, the more you and your horse will come to resemble the ideal picture of harmony and ease as riding partners.

The Rider's Training Scale

I don't want to get into too much detail about what you can already find in many other books. Nonetheless, I think it is important to at least touch upon the basic points that everyone needs to know when riding dressage.

The training of the dressage rider is divided into the following categories:

- The dressage (basic) seat
- Administration of the aids
- "Feel"
- Effectiveness of the aids

The Dressage (Basic) Seat

A prerequisite for effective aids is a correct seat. There are three types of seats that are commonly correct in different English riding situations: the *dressage seat*, the *forward seat*, and the *racing/jockey seat*. I will not address the racing seat in this book; I only mention it here because I feel it can be helpful for your overall "feel" and position to occasionally practice riding in this position.

In Germany, where I ride and train, the *dressage seat* is the first seat taught to new riders, and it is the seat that is most frequently used when riding. For this reason it is also called the *basic seat*. This is what it entails:

- The rider sits without tension in the middle of the saddle. Her weight is distributed evenly on both seat bones. The weight-bearing surface of the seat is comprised of the two seat bones and the space in between them.
- The rider's thighs are slightly back and slightly turned in.
- The thigh position enables the knees to be low with a slight bend.
- The calves angle more or less back (toward the tail of the horse), bringing the rider's heels under her hips. (The angle

will be more with longer legs than with shorter legs.) The calves remain in contact with the horse's sides.

- The feet should be parallel to the horse's sides with the ball of each on the respective stirrup iron. The heel stretches slightly downward so that it is the lowest part of the leg, and the ankle must remain elastic.
- The upper body should be straight but not held unnaturally erect. To maintain the stability of the seat and position the rider must have a healthy dose of "positive" muscle tension—but not so much as to detract from the body's relaxation and the suppleness of the seat.
- Correct upper body position allows the rider's hips to follow the horse's movement, enabling the horse and rider to move together harmoniously. The rider follows the movement that originates from the horse and swings with it. Note: An over-exaggerated "following" motion from the rider disturbs the horse and is incorrect.
- The head should be carried straight, and the rider should look ahead in the direction of travel.
- The shoulders should be held back—without tension—with the upper arms hanging down from them.
- The elbows are bent and lightly touching the rider's upper body.
- The hands, carried in front of the rider's body, are closed in relaxed "fists" with thumbs on top and slightly bent (in the shape of a pitched roof).

While striving to achieve an "optically ideal" seat (it looks good), it can't be forgotten that what may appear to be correct is worthless if it is not functional. By this I mean the seat must be free of "negative" tension: It should be maintained with mini- mal effort while remaining supple and able to move with the horse's motion.

Three Important Points

1 When viewed from the side, the rider's shoulder, hip, and heel should be vertically aligned.

2 When viewed from the side, there should be a straight line from the horse's mouth, through the rider's hand, to the elbow.

3 When viewed from behind, the rider's spine should form a straight vertical line that is centered on the horse's spine.

In comparison, the *forward seat* is necessary in certain situations, such as when riding young horses with limited strength and conditioning, when riding over cavalletti, or when going over jumps. The forward seat is characterized by the following:

- The stirrups are shortened to accommodate the riding situation (for example, if you are riding over cavalletti, small fences, or large fences). This affords the rider's legs more security and allows the ankles to absorb the movement of the rider and the horse as they stretch downward.
- Unlike the vertical upper body position of the dressage seat (see p. 1), in the forward seat, the upper body is held at a forward angle, with the rider flexed at the hips. As with the dressage seat, the rider's upper body must remain elastic.
- The rider can remain in the saddle in the forward seat, but she comes out of the saddle over jumps.
- The arms are carried further to the front of the rider's body in the forward seat (as compared to the dressage seat), with the hands in front of the withers and on either side of the horse's neck.

2

Unlike the dressage seat, the forward seat requires the rider's knees, calves, and heels support her weight.

Riders with a good sense of feel are equipped to quickly adjust to riding new horses, react appropriately in critical situations, and complete challenging exercises and combinations of movements.

Administration of the Aids

While in the saddle, the rider communicates with the horse using a language of succinct signals. These signals are called aids. There are several forms of aids, including *seat*, *leg*, and *rein* aids, and they are listed here in order of importance. (Note: I describe all these aids in more detail on the pages ahead—see the references below.)

Depending on what the rider is asking of the horse:
- The *seat aids* can be administered or withheld on both sides, or administered on one side (see p. 10).
- The *leg aids* can be administered with a forward-driving effect, a sideways-driving effect, or a passive, "guarding" effect (see p. 12).
- The *rein aids* can be used with a following, holding, sideways-guiding, guarding, or giving effect (see p. 13).

"Feel"

Over time, experienced riders develop a good sense of *feel*. This doesn't mean being especially gentle all the time but rather always reacting with the appropriate degree and strength of aids, as well as the right combination of aids and the use of aids at the right time. Additionally, riders should develop a feel for anticipating potential "negative" tension in the horse and addressing it, and its causes, in a timely manner.

Effectiveness of the Aids

The ability to ride with feel and with aids that are invisible to an observer is the crown jewel of the training process for the rider, although the truly good rider never stops learning. *Effective aids* are aids that are applied from a correct and supple seat, using a good sense of feel to determine their necessary intensity and duration. The aids should always be applied in conjunction with each other and never in isolation in order to achieve better quality of movement, suppleness, and willingness in the horse.

The *driving aids* should always take priority over the *restraining aids*!

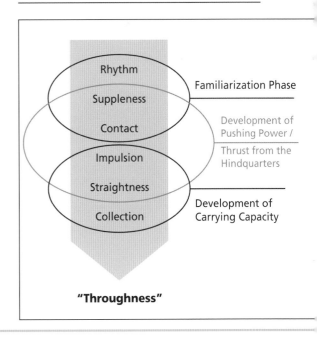

Rhythm

Suppleness

Contact

Impulsion

Straightness

Collection

Familiarization Phase

Development of Pushing Power / Thrust from the Hindquarters

Development of Carrying Capacity

"Throughness"

The Classical Training Scale

I must take this moment to stress the importance of this chapter and its content. I know no one likes to study before mounting her horse, but the Classical Training Scale is a well-thought-out system in which one stepping stone is built upon the next, and all parts work in conjunction with each other. It should really be internalized by all riders and referred to continually in the course of their riding career. In the following section I will discuss the attributes of each point on the Classical Training Scale:

Rhythm describes the horse's footfalls in all three gaits, which should occur in a consistent pattern in time and in placement. Every step or stride at the walk, trot, and canter should maintain a consistent tempo, meaning that each stride within one gait takes the same amount of time and covers the same amount of ground. If this is not the case, a disturbance of the horse's rhythm has occurred, and this is referred to as a *rhythm irregularity*. The correct rhythm entails a four-beat walk, a two-beat trot, and a three-beat canter.

The horse should be *physically supple* and *mentally relaxed*, but this does not mean that he is tired or "floppy," rather he should possess a "positive" tension in his body. Clear signs of **suppleness** include a pleasant or calm facial expression; a closed, softly chewing mouth; gentle snorting; a swinging back; and a tail that

I allow Adele to stretch. She is willingly lengthening and lowering her neck. As this exercise continues, the horse should be encouraged to stretch her neck even longer as she becomes more supple.

Even on a turn or curved line, the horse's hind feet should directly follow the tracks of the front feet, demonstrating the horse is really straight. This photo clearly shows Adele lowering her inside hip. She is working well with her hind end, nicely bending the joints of her left hip, stifle, and hock.

sways slightly from side to side. At all times the horse should be able to stretch forward and downward if asked.

An honest **contact**, in which the horse's forehead is slightly in front of the vertical, is obtained by sending the horse forward into an elastic and momentarily "holding" hand. Contact is a prerequisite for the horse to be able to carry himself in a frame and move in a balanced way under the rider.

Ideal Position

The ideal head and neck position, in which the horse's poll is the highest point and the horse's forehead is slightly in front of the vertical, need not be strictly adhered to at all times. Horses that are equipped with a neck of an ideal length and shape, and with a "clean" throatlatch area, will find it easy to maintain this optimal neck carriage.

However, very few horses are perfect. I work the horse that tends to come above the bit a little deeper (but only very slightly!) in the neck, and in the case of the horse that tends to curl up and shorten his neck, I insist that he always carries himself in front of the vertical. In such cases, I only ask the horse to maintain the *ideal* neck position *some of the time*. With all horses, whatever their conformation and tendencies—and especially young horses—it is most important that they are always willing and able to stretch forward and downward when asked.

Impulsion refers to the positive effect the activity of the hindquarters has on the overall quality of the horse's movement. The horse's hind legs take energetic forward-and-upward steps, carrying their movement forward over the horse's "swinging" back. Suppleness and an increasing degree of "throughness" allow the horse's movement to become optimal.

Straightness entails bringing the horse's forehand in line with his hindquarters so that his hind feet step in the same track as his forefeet. When straightness is achieved, the horse's body works evenly on both sides, with no one part taxed more heavily than others. This improves the horse's overall health and soundness, as well as his general rideability.

When a degree of **collection** is attained, the three main joints of the hindquarters (hips, stifles, and hocks) bend more and increase the amount of weight they carry. They step further under the horse's center of gravity, compressing the horse's frame and giving the impression that the horse is more compact. The collected horse becomes more "uphill" from back to front. This allows his forelegs to move more freely and his movement becomes more cadenced. The horse moves in self-carriage.

"Throughness" is the positive result of work on the elements of the Classical Training Scale. A horse that is "through" immediately and obediently responds to the rider's aids: He lengthens or shortens his frame upon request, and he is ready to collect or extend his stride when asked.

Although he's not naturally equipped with the most impressive movement, with gym-nasticizing exercises, Isidor has obtained an attractive collected trot with hind legs that step well under his center of gravity and sufficient uphill balance with his poll as the highest point.

The Aids:
The Rider's Toolbox

In the last chapter I mentioned the different types of aids (see p. 3). Since the aids are what allow you to communicate with your mount, it is important to have a basic understanding of them. In addition, there are specific considerations to keep in mind when applying them:

- Use a friendly "tone": You wouldn't appreciate being rudely accosted during a normal, everyday conversation with another person. The dialogue between horse and rider should be just as soft and respectful. Of course, the rider may need to make her point clearly when there is a disagreement, but afterward it is important to return to a positive tone.

- Note when discipline is necessary: When your horse won't do something that you know he can do, or when he is simply not paying attention and doesn't react, appropriate and timely punishment may be in order. This *does not* mean brutal application of the whip or yanking on the reins. A very clearly given aid can be enough of a disciplinary action. Check that your correction was effective by testing the horse—ask him to respond to a "normal" aid again.

- Don't give endless aids: Imagine what it is like when your conversation partner blabbers at you endlessly about trivial matters. Eventually your brain "shuts off" and you tune him or her out. This happens with horses, as well. If you give constant, monotone, repetitive aids, your horse will become desensitized to them and no longer "hear" you. Thus, it is important to ride with aids applied with logical timing and meaning.

- Cultivate reactions to subtle aids: Do you feel like you need an oxygen mask after your warm-up because your horse won't travel for even a few strides by himself and without you "pushing" or "carrying" him along? This problem must be addressed and can't be solved just by riding around and around the arena. The horse must be taught to respond immediately to your aids. For example, only use a light, brief leg aid on your horse. If the horse ignores it, repeat the aid with the same intensity. *Do not* defer to a longer, stronger squeeze. If reinforcement is necessary, use the spur or the whip right behind the calf, or on the horse's shoulder. Do not hold your horse back with the reins when making this correction, even if he is likely to react explosively—a "wake up" is the desired effect!

- Understand the absence of aids as a reward: Just as an exaggerated or repeated aid is in some ways a kind of punishment for your horse, the absence of aids is a kind of reward. Become passive between aids to maintain your horse's relaxed and happy attitude.

- Avoid excessive use of strength when giving aids: Firstly, riding with such overt use of strength does not look good, and secondly, exaggerated use of strength is usually accompanied by muscle tension, which makes a relaxed and supple seat impossible. This has a negative influence on your horse's own suppleness and movement.

- Obedience is still key: Although we strive for harmony between horse and rider, in the end the horse must be obedient to the rider when under saddle. This can be compared to what it is like to raise a young child: When the child whines and disobeys, it is important that the parent has the last word. Then the child learns to see the parent as a consistent authority figure and accepts his or her guidance.

Seat and Weight Aids

There are different ways to employ the seat and weight aids:

- They can be *administered on both sides* of the horse.
- They can be *withheld on both sides* of the horse.
- They can be *administered on one side* of the horse.

In a dressage (basic) seat, the seat aids are *administered on both sides of the horse* most of the time, when traveling in a straight line. There is a range of intensity of strength used with the seat aids. When giving a half-halt, for example, the rider's pelvis can give a short pressure in the direction of the saddle pommel. When being passive (not consciously giving a seat aid), the rider's seat still has an effect as her core swings with the horse's movement.

The seat aids are also sometimes *withheld on both sides*—for example, in rising trot. In this case the application of the aids alternates: withheld on both sides, then administered on both sides, and so on. Also, when riding a transition from the halt to the trot or the walk to the trot, the rider slightly lightens the seat on both sides to free the horse's back and allow it to move forward. This enables the horse's hind legs to step more easily under his center of gravity.

The seat aids are *administered on one side* during turns and lateral movements. In my experience these aids vary according to their intended purpose. When riding a curved line, such as a corner or a volte (a small, circular school figure with a diameter of 6, 8, or 10 meters), or when riding a lateral movement, the rider's *inside hip* ("inside" the bend) should be pushed forward, but the *outside seat bone* still carries some weight. As the inside hip moves forward, the rider's *inside leg* stays forward in a position to send the horse forward. Imagine that you are standing on the ground with your feet evenly placed. If you take one step forward with your left foot, your left hip will come forward in front of your right hip. Your right leg—and actually your entire right side—will logically be back behind your left, just as if your leg were in the "guarding" position on the horse. So, to ride a turn, just "take a step forward" with your inside leg!

To ride a leg-yield or a turn-on-the-forehand you use a one-sided seat aid (among other aids). However, unlike when you use the aid to ride a turn as described above (where the inside seat bone moves *forward*), when you perform a leg-yield or turn-on-the-forehand, the seat bone works by moving in a *forward-and-diagonal* direction to push the horse forward at the desired angle.

Imagine that the seat of your saddle is the face of a clock. In front of you (the pommel) is twelve o'clock and behind you (the cantle) is six o'clock. When riding straight ahead, both seat bones roll forward in rhythm with the horse from six o'clock to twelve o'clock. When riding a leg-yield to the left, your inside seat bone (the right, in this case, as the horse is bent away from the direction of travel), which is also more weighted, should move from about five o'clock toward eleven o'clock in rhythm with the horse. (Consider in contrast if it moved along the three o'clock to nine o'clock line—that would move you too much to the side and not enough forward.) As another example, when riding a volte to the left, the inside seat bone (the left, here) would move from about six o'clock toward ten o'clock.

I am looking ahead around the turn. This automatically brings my inside shoulder ("inside" the bend) back and my inside hip forward.

When riding a bending line it is crucial to look in the direction in which you wish to ride. Then the rider's weight is automatically correctly distributed for the turn, and the inside hip and seat bone naturally come forward.

Leg Aids

There are three types of leg aids:
- Forward driving
- Forward-sideways driving
- "Guarding"

The rider's leg should be positioned *at the girth* for the *forward-driving* aid. This means that the front edge of the upper part of the boot should be near the back edge of the girth. The rider's calf should not permanently press into the horse's side, but rather should maintain a very light contact and "breathe" with the horse. When a leg aid is needed, the light contact increases for an instant. Often the horse responds to the aid only after the rider's leg has relaxed again. The *forward-sideways driving* leg is positioned a hands-width *behind the girth*. This

Correct positioning of the *forward-sideways driving* leg and *guarding* leg.

leg aid is used to direct the horse's hind leg on the same side to cross over the other hind leg, such as in leg-yielding and turn-on-the-forehand. This aid should be given in rhythm with the horse's movement: For maximum effect, it should be applied at the moment in which the horse's hind leg lifts off the ground.

The *"guarding"* leg is also positioned a

Correct positioning of the *forward-driving* leg.

hands-width *behind the girth*. It prevents the hindquarters from falling out and controls the degree of angle or sideways movement created by the rider's opposing forward-sideways driving aid, as well as the degree of lateral bend.

The exact position of the legs is again a result of the positioning of the rider's hips. The rider's *outside seat bone* (outside the bend) is *not* additionally weighted when the rider is using the *inside leg* and *inside seat bone* as an aid. The outside hip and seat bone stay slightly back behind the inside. Since each leg "falls" down from the hip, the outside leg automatically lies further back than the inside, in its guarding position.

Rein Aids

With the reins the rider can:
- "Take" and "give"
- "Hold"
- "Guard"
- Guide the horse sideways

"Taking" and *"giving" on the reins* should always go together so that *taking* only lasts for a brief moment and is always followed by *giving*. When needed, the taking can be repeated immediately, and also more firmly (see more on this below). Riders must take and give on the reins frequently since they comprise part of the aids necessary for a half-halt. (Interestingly, you can usually only see the effect of taking during the giving phase of the half-halt.) Taking and giving on the reins is also used to ride a transition to the halt, and to flex and bend the horse.

To *take* on the reins, the rider's fists close more firmly on the reins. If that is not enough, the rider's wrists, which are usu-

ally relaxed and elastic, can bend slightly. If flexion and bend in the horse is desired for a longer duration, the *flexing rein* (on the *inside* of the bend) can be shortened. Then the rider can take and give with the slightly shorter rein.

To *give*, closed fists can be slightly opened, bent wrists can be straightened, and the shorter rein (when applicable) can be lengthened so that it is even with the other rein.

A *"holding"* rein can be used to correct problems in the contact. If the horse is "against the hand" or above the bit, a holding rein creates a limit to the outward or upward movement of the horse's head. The rider keeps her hand in position and relaxes the fist only when the horse has stopped pulling against the bit and has softened his poll and neck downward. I would like to emphasize that this rein aid is never to be used in isolation, but always in conjunction with the forward-driving leg and seat aids (see pp. 12 and 10)!

The *"guarding"* rein works opposite of the flexing rein (see above). It prevents the flexing rein from positioning the horse's neck too much to the side, which would cause the opposite shoulder to fall out. When the horse's right side is his hollow side, for example, then when tracking right, the use of the (left) guarding rein is crucial in riding a turn or corner.

The *sideways guiding rein* or *opening rein* is often used with young horses to guide them through a turn, for example. But the sideways guiding rein can also be used with more advanced horses to help them learn a new movement, such as the half-pass. To turn using the sideways guiding rein, the hand is moved from its normal position out to the side, guiding the horse's head and neck onto the desired path of travel.

In this photo of a volte you can clearly see the use of the outside rein to keep the horse's shoulder from falling out. Despite this, Isidor is still slightly tilting his poll.

The rider's hand must not move backward as it "opens" out to the side—it should stay on the same plane on which it is normally positioned.

The Half-Halt

The half-halt is the rider's most useful tool. It is comprised of a combination of seat/weight, leg, and rein aids, used together so that the aids "package" the horse. Half-halts are used to:

- Establish and improve connection in the horse's body.
- Improve carriage and degree of collection.
- Prepare for an upcoming movement.
- Ride transitions within and among the gaits.

The individual aids for the half-halt are adjusted depending upon the particular half-halt's desired effect. For example, if you want to notify your horse of an approaching turn, use your seat and leg aids to drive into the outside, holding rein (see p. 13), while the inside rein asks for flexion (see p. 13).

If you want to put your horse on the aids and on the bit so that he gives at the poll, drive him forward with both legs and seat bones evenly, and alternate taking and giving evenly on both reins. The *taking* part of the rein aid tells the horse to give at the poll, while the *giving* prevents him from becoming resistant. These aids must be used constantly and alternately. Note that the strength of the rein aid necessary to put the horse on the bit to begin with is firmer than the more subtle aids used to remind him to maintain the frame.

A half-halt is essentially "packaging" the horse with the weight, leg, and rein-aids. This four-year-old horse already responds correctly to the half-halt by shortening his frame and stepping well underneath himself with his hind legs. This moment shows the *taking* phase of the half-halt; in the next moment, which is the *giving* phase, the horse's nose should reach forward more than is shown here.

The Arena:
The Rider's Workshop

Dressage practice typically takes place in an indoor arena or an outdoor dressage ring. This is of course logical, because these spaces have been specifically designed and measured out to facilitate riding accurate dressage figures and movements. However, riders need to remember they are not actually required to *always* ride in the ring!

Areas Suitable for Training

Regardless of where you ride, the circumstances should be appropriate. The footing shouldn't be too deep or too hard, and it should be free of holes and debris. When applicable, the fencing or enclosure should be safe and secure, and the presence of "outside" distractions that may affect the horse should be limited.

These days, many larger boarding stables are equipped with indoor arenas. The indoor arena is an optimal choice for the more timid rider, as well as when working the young or difficult horse, because it is fully enclosed and offers a low level of visual stimuli to potentially distract or frighten the horse.

Another benefit often found with indoor arenas is having mirrors mounted on the walls, which enable the rider to observe and analyze herself and her horse, making corrections in position when necessary.

An enclosed outdoor ring can offer a first step toward "freedom" for horse and rider. Standard outdoor ring dimensions are usually larger than those of an indoor arena, so they are well suited for riding long, straight lines at a nicely forward pace, perhaps even in a forward (jumping) position (see p. 2). This kind of exercise improves the horse's natural desire to go forward.

The horse is exposed to more stimuli in an outdoor ring than in an indoor arena. This offers the rider an opportunity to school and improve the horse's obedience while performing dressage movements. Adequate fencing around an outdoor ring can give the timid rider confidence during outdoor work. In addition, a secure fence line helps "support" and contain the horse as he responds to the rider's aids. Note that it is wise to check that your horse really is on the aids and under control by (at least) occasionally riding him without the support of the fence—that is, in the open, on the trail, or in an outdoor ring specifically geared toward dressage practice. Often the latter is of specific dimensions and bordered only by a very low fence, if by anything at all. Only work your horse in an outdoor dressage arena once he is under control in an enclosed arena—it is not a suitable schooling area for starting a young horse, for example. Not only do green horses benefit from the support of a fence or wall, but riding untrained horses in an unenclosed space poses a safety risk.

Riding in an outdoor dressage arena without a high fence increases the difficulty of movements ridden along the track, such as shoulder-in (see p. 119). A horse that is primarily accustomed to the support of a wall or fence will show his uncertainty in such a situation by wavering in his path of travel. This demonstrates that the horse must improve his response to the rider's aids!

As mentioned on p. 25, it is also possible to school dressage out on the trails. Shoulder-in, leg-yield, transitions, and halts can all be practiced on a trail ride. If a suitable field is available (and this may only be at certain times of year, depending on footing) you can potentially ride through all the dressage movements outside of the typical

You can avoid causing your horse unnecessary stress in "strange" or hectic environments, such as horse shows, by introducing him to schooling in a variety of new and different places beforehand.

arena environment. Experiencing undulations underfoot improves the horse's movement, and changing location offers both horse and rider scenic variety while giving the rider a chance to learn the horse's reaction to new situations.

The 20- by 40-Meter Arena

There are two traditionally accepted sizes for a dressage arena: 20 by 40 meters and 20 by 60 meters. Since so many dressage move-ments are oriented by the arena letters, I would like to discuss the measurements of these dressage rings and distances between points within them. Until a rider has mas-tered the most commonly ridden dressage figures, it is advisable to ride them at the let-ters. Once the rider has internalized the size

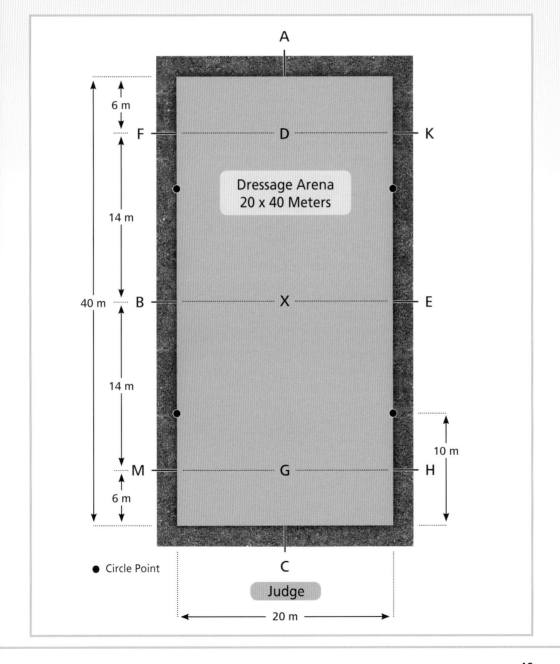

and shape of the movements and can ride them accurately at a letter, then she should feel free to ride them at any location.

The 20- by 40-meter (or "small") arena is divided in half lengthwise by the centerline, which runs from A to C, meaning that each track on the long side is 10 meters from the centerline. A 10-meter volte from the track should exactly touch the centerline. A 5-meter, shallow-loop serpentine entails riding from the track to the quarterline, *not* the centerline. The quarterline runs the length of the long side of the arena, half way between the track and the centerline.

The small arena is also divided into two, 20-meter halves by an invisible line the length of the short side running from E to B and crossing the centerline at X. A circle beginning at A or C on either short side reaches this imaginary line. The circle should touch the track on each long side at the *circle point*—a point exactly 10 meters from the closest corner. A circle beginning on the track at B or E will reach as far as the imaginary line connecting the two circle points closest to C and the two circle points closest to A.

The 20- by 40-meter arena can be divided into four, 10-meter sections by an invisible line connecting the circle points closest to C, an invisible line running from E to B, and one connecting the circle points closest to A. You can use these points for orientation when riding a four-loop serpentine through the ring, for example.

Tip

While the order of the arena letters may seem random, they can be remembered with this mnemonic device: All King Edward's Horses Can Make Big Fences.

The 20- by 60-Meter Arena

The 20- by 60-meter (or large) arena is not as clearly laid out as the small arena. In order to ride many figures and movements—such as circles, serpentines, and lateral movements—the rider must be familiar with the distances between letters and from the letters to the corners. Don't think that accuracy isn't important because even at shows you can see many riders who don't ride the figures and movements accurately! Take a moment to analyze the layout of the ring so that this won't happen to you.

A 20-meter circle starting at C or A must reach out as far as 2 meters past R and S or P and V, since these letters are 18 meters from the corner. Riding a circle at E or B, among other locations, also requires the rider to hit unmarked points of the arena.

When riding a four-loop serpentine through the large arena, the line from E to B bisects the movement, just as in the small arena. The second loop ends and the third loop begins on this line. In a four-loop serpentine, each loop is 15 meters wide. The first loop becomes the second loop on a line parallel to the short side, not at R and S or P and V, but again, at an unmarked point.

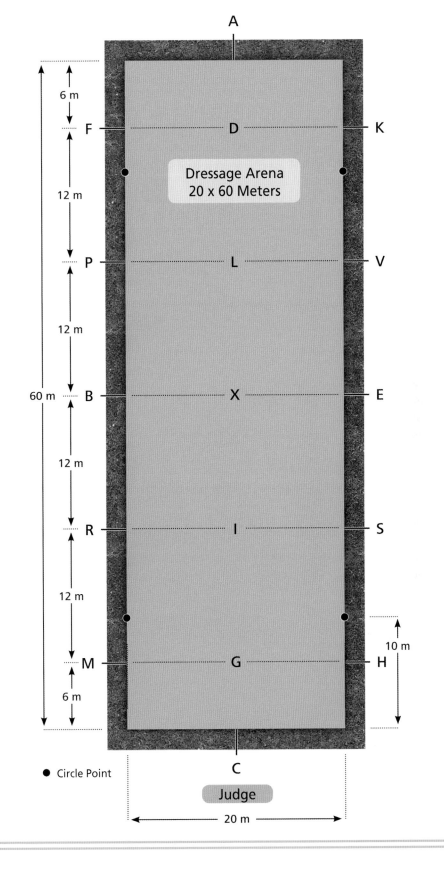

The Movements and Their Variations: Training the Horse Appropriately

There is a common repertoire of exercises used in daily dressage training, such as transitions and serpentines, for example. Later on, lateral work and flying changes are added to the program. These movements are included in dressage tests at competitions; however, don't make the mistake of drilling for the sole purpose of competing. The dressage test is really intended to tell you if you are on the right training path with your horse. It acts as a milestone in your progress together. A horse that is trained in accordance with the Classical Training Scale (see p. 4) will produce correct movements as a result of his rider's careful attention to his progress and her willingness to adjust her focus and lesson program as necessary. Correct movements are *not* the result of practicing each movement hundreds of times.

There are a limited number of "classical" figures that can be used at the lower levels of dressage training, including circles, voltes, and serpentines. While you can't reinvent the wheel, with a little creativity, you can make a series of useful and interesting exercises out of these basic dressage figures that also improve the horse's "throughness" (see p. 6). I introduce some of my favorite versions of these exercises in the pages ahead. There are no limits set on the possible variations: These exercises can and should be endlessly modified to keep the horse's daily work interesting to him. While at first you may find that it is not as easy as it sounds to ride a "basic" exercise correctly, with practice you will be able to combine various simple elements together to create a series of effective exercises.

Basis for a Training Plan

Just as the horse's training is carefully built up over time using the Classical Training Scale, your daily "lesson plan" can be structured so that each step builds upon the step before it.

Over years of dressage training, the horse's *pushing power*, and then later *carrying capacity*, is developed and improved.

Adele in a working canter while warming up in a long frame.

23

Adele again, this time shown during the work phase of a schooling session in collected canter, developing straightness.

Once a horse is trained for under-saddle work, each individual ride should be divided into a *warm-up phase*, a *work phase*, and a *cool-down phase*. At the beginning of each ride you should take the time to walk the horse for 10 to 15 minutes to warm and prepare the horse's muscles for further work. Initial trot and canter work also counts as part of the warm-up—this is when the focus should be on the first three elements of the Training Scale (rhythm, suppleness, and contact—see p. 4). The work phase, depending upon the level of the horse, will then address straightness, impulsion, and collection. At the end of the ride, the horse should be allowed to mentally and physical-

ly relax. He should be allowed one last loose and relaxed trot, and then he should walk until his rate of breathing is back to normal. It is a good idea to have a plan for your daily riding session, but you should not have the same plan every day! Change your points of focus and ride in different locations—variety is beneficial to both you and the horse. In addition, ensure your horse's happiness by giving him a chance to move around other than while under saddle (regular turnout), and allow him social contact with other horses for at least a little while each day if he doesn't live in a herd situation.

A Personalized Training "Guidebook"

As previously mentioned, the rider should have a clear idea of what to work on before starting each day's training session. Do you want to refine your transitions? Have you done strenuous collected work several days in a row and now want to give your horse a day of suppling and stretching? Or do you want to ride smaller circles and voltes than you and your horse have tried before? It doesn't matter what your goal is or how "small" or "big" it may seem, as long as you have a goal in mind. Remember: It is better to reach a very small goal than to be stumped by an overly ambitious one.

When you are unsuccessful at introducing a new lesson or fail to accomplish what you set out to do with your horse, take a step back to the level at which you and your horse are confident, and then start again, but this time take smaller steps toward your goal.

- As previously stated, in order to accomplish any goal, you must have a plan. Know your horse and any difficulties he will likely have with what you are asking, and be prepared with ways to correct him.
- Don't struggle with the same problem every day if you can't solve it quickly. Revisit it after practicing other movements to keep your relationship with your horse positive.
- It is commendable to always ride with perfect position and invisible aids. However, occasions may arise that require a momentary departure from the ideal, and less-than-subtle aids in order to get a point across. This of course does not mean that you shouldn't always strive for the optimum.
- I can remember riding lessons that I could set my watch to, with my instructor always asking for the canter or leg-yield at the exact same point in the session. Spare yourself and your horse this monotony. A ride doesn't inherently need to last for a full hour. Many people mistakenly believe that meaningful training cannot be accomplished in less than 60 minutes. Riders who pay for riding lessons or training with a professional often want a full 60 minutes for their money and are simply not satisfied with less, even when a breakthrough is realized or a goal met within 30 or 40 minutes. I personally go by the rule that I will ride for whatever amount of time it takes to attain an *acceptable* result. This could occur after 45 minutes, or some days, not until 75 minutes have passed, but it *never* means continuing to drill until the horse has achieved something *excellent*. Riding unnecessarily long will only tire the horse, which can have a nega-

Don't just ride "laps" around the arena. Incorporate suppling exercises that are good for you and your horse. Note: At the moment this photo was taken, Isidor is clearly behind the vertical due to a lot of flexion around a turn. This is not a problem if it only occurs for a moment as part of a correction: In this case, the cause was a firm rein aid used to increase flexion.

tive effect that lasts days. This is neither productive for his willingness to work nor good for his overall well-being.
- Avoid simply riding around and around the arena on the track, even if you want to have an easier or less intense training session. Riding a set number of "laps" only serves to wear out and bore your horse. You should enjoy your horse—not ride him into the ground. If you want a less serious, more relaxing day with your horse, consider going for a trail ride, longeing him for a short period, or riding a few suppling exercises that are easy and beneficial for both you and your horse.

Turning Basic Dressage Figures into Creative Exercises

In the pages ahead I describe 55 exercises in detail, along with a plan for how to ride each one.

First I explain the path of travel for the exercise (*Where You Go*), then I describe its purpose and benefits (*Why You Do It*), and finally I explain the aids so that you can try it yourself (*Here's How*). I also mention common difficulties that you may encounter (*Having Problems?*). Note that while I haven't mentioned problems for *all* of the exercises, that doesn't mean that problems can't occur. Similar problems tend to occur in related exercises, so I haven't restated them for each exercise when that is the case.

I have also provided a diagram to illustrate each exercise and give you a quick "at-a-glance" idea of what to do. Below is a key to the symbols I have used in the diagrams ahead.

Riding on the Track and in the Corners

Riding any kind of turn requires the horse to be on the aids to ensure he accepts increased weight on the inside hind leg. Although they may seem trivial, the corners of the dressage ring count as turns! Think of it this way: Every corner is equivalent to riding a quarter of a volte. The diameter of this volte depends on the horse's level of training. At First Level and under, the corner should be ridden as a quarter of a 10-meter volte. This should be possible even for horses that don't compete and are "only" ridden for pleasure. At Second and Third levels the corners should be ridden as quarters of an 8-meter volte, and for Fourth Level and above, as 6-meter voltes.

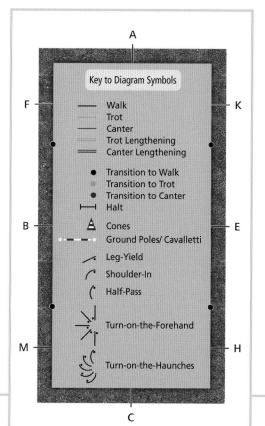

Here we see good bend and flexion in the corner of the arena. I should shorten my inside rein so that my hand doesn't need to be brought as far back as it is here.

Correct Corners

Where You Go

Trot on the track down the long side. Before reaching the short side, ride a transition to walk. At first, ride the transition with plenty of space before the corner. As you repeat the exercise, however, gradually decrease the distance between the transition and the corner. Ride through the corner in walk. Trot directly after the corner, and try riding the next corner in trot.

Why You Do It

It is common to see riders straining to ride complicated figures accurately while neglecting their corners. Their horses "fall through the corners," for example, with a complete lack of bend through the body, become unsteady in the contact, or lose either their rhythm or their impulsion because their riders attempt to ride as deep into a corner as possible.

After only a few trips around the ring, focusing on *correct corners*, you will already notice a positive change in your horse. A half-halt or a full transition to walk before the corner prepares the horse for the turn by increasing the weight he carries on his hindquarters. Riding the first corner in walk gives the rider time to concentrate on the aids and to correctly flex and bend the horse. In trot or canter the horse may try to evade, as it is more work to travel correctly through a corner. And, by the time the rider attempts to address the evasion, the corner has already passed!

It is important to ride correct corners because each corner is a test of whether the horse can maintain rhythm and connection in a turn. Each corner also improves his lateral bend and the activity of his inside hind leg.

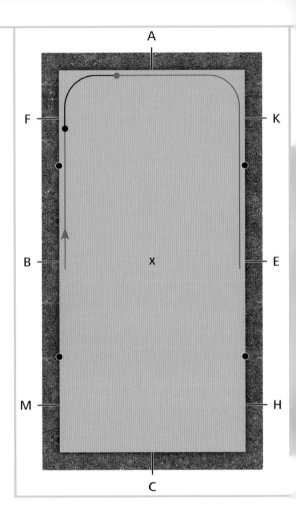

Here's How

1 Trot down the long side of the arena on the track. As you approach the first corner of the short side, use half-halts to prepare for a transition to walk. At this point the horse should not have noticeable flexion toward the inside of the arena.

2 Half-halt to the walk *before* the corner. Maintain your rein length since you will trot again right away.

3 Push your inside hip (toward the inside of the arena) forward. Apply your inside leg at the girth, to drive the horse forward, and maintain your outside leg in the guarding position to prevent the

horse's hindquarters from falling out (p. 13). Use the inside rein to ask the horse to flex to the inside while the outside rein allows for the flexion to happen. Note, however, the outside rein should *not* be slack, or the horse will "bulge out" with his shoulder, and the contact and connection will be unsteady after the corner.

4   In the corner, bring your inside shoulder back (which causes the outside shoulder to be slightly forward). Slightly flex your inside wrist toward the horse's withers. Neither of your hands should move significantly forward (toward the horse's ears) or backward (toward your torso).

5   Upon reaching the deepest part of the corner, "give" with the inside rein so the horse leaves the corner straight on the short side. The horse should be predominantly on the outside rein as he comes out of the corner.

6   After the corner, ride straight on the short side (again *without* flexing to the inside). Both your seat bones should be equally weighted, while both your legs hang down at the girth, driving the horse straight forward. Both reins should be of equal length as you ask for a transition back to trot with a half-halt to prepare, followed by quick pressure with both calves and "giving" with both reins equally.

7   Before the second corner on the short side, balance the horse with a half-halt and ride through the corner as described at the beginning of this exercise, but this time in trot. Repeat the exercise in both directions, riding the first corner in walk and the second in trot, gradually shortening the distance between your transition to walk on the long side and the first corner.

As you come out of the first corner on the short side, ride straight and prepare to pick up the trot before coming to the second corner.

Having Problems?

● *You and your horse ride a correct corner in walk but can't seem to do it in trot.* When this is the case, walk before every corner, or walk through the whole short side. Over time, gradually decrease the number of walk steps so you ride your downward transition to walk increasingly closer to beginning the corner and trot again sooner following it.

- *Your horse comes off the bit in the corner or leans on the inside rein*. This problem indicates he is probably not active enough with his inside hind leg. Create more energy within the half-halt as you balance your horse before the corner, and "give" more clearly with the inside rein so that your horse has to carry himself. Another cause of this problem can be too much flexion to the inside. Keep a firmer contact with the outside rein and ask for less flexion with the inside rein. Aim to flex the horse only enough to barely see his inside eye and the edge of his inside nostril.

- *Your horse goes very deep into the corner (of his own accord) and then comes out "wavering and wiggling."* This is a classic case of "bulging out" through the shoulder. The outside rein must be steadier. Make a conscious effort to ride less deep into the corner so that you control the horse's path of travel so that he doesn't get literally "off track."

- *Your horse loses rhythm or impulsion in the corner.* The diameter (size) of the quarter volte you have chosen to ride may be too challenging for your horse's level of training (see p. 27). "Flatten out" the corner for now. Gradually ride deeper into the corner over time, only increasing the depth (decreasing the size of the quarter volte) when the horse stays rhythmical and maintains impulsion.

Turn Left, Turn Right

Where You Go

Trot along the arena track, tracking left. Before reaching E, half-halt and make a downward transition to the walk. At E make a 90-degree *left turn*. Immediately following the turn, trot on again. Ride straight toward B. Before B, transition to walk, and at B make a 90-degree *right turn* onto the track, now going in the opposite direction. Once you are on the track, pick up the trot again.

Why You Do It

This exercise combines *riding transitions* with *riding turns*. It improves and tests the horse's lateral bend and therefore his straightness. It also improves the degree to which the horse is *on the aids*, especially the outside aids (outside the bend), and his "throughness." Including walk transitions in this exercise teaches riders to ride the figure more accurately.

Here's How

1 Trot down the long side of the arena, tracking left.

2 Before you reach E, ride a transition to walk.

3 At E turn left. Ride a *correct corner* as learned in Exercise 1 (see p. 28).

4 After the turn, straighten your horse with the right (outside) rein so that the line from E to B is straight (and not a serpentine)!

5 Ride an upward transition to trot and ride straight ahead toward B. Make sure both your seat bones are equally weighted and both calves are at the girth, sending the horse forward, so the horse is straight between both reins.

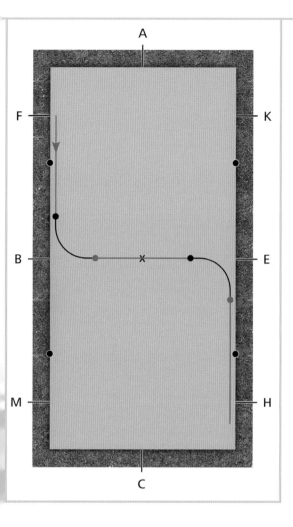

A

F — — K

B — — X — — E

M — — H

C

Having Problems?

- *Your horse "falls out," missing the invisible straight line connecting E and B.* When this is the case, make your turn earlier. Your horse's "turning radius" will vary according to his level of training. You will be able to make smaller turns (smaller quarter-voltes) with increased practice. Make sure that your outside rein and guarding outside leg are there to limit the size of the turn and support your horse as you go out of the corner and onto the straight line.

- *It is hard to flex your horse to the inside before the turn.* Take more time to prepare before the turn. Ride the transition to the walk with enough time to address the need for flexion, using many half-halts; giving and taking clearly on the inside rein. Return to Exercise 1 if needed (see p. 28): There the horse is more "enclosed" and "supported" by the track and arena fence or wall.

- *Your line from E to B is a diagonal or curved line instead of a straight one.* Pay close attention to riding your turns as correct corners and straightening your horse directly afterward. After the first turn, use a balancing half-halt to "package" your horse from back to front, and limit his path of travel with your outside rein so that he stays straight when you ask him to trot energetically forward.

6 Before reaching B—after you have only trotted a few strides—ride a transition to walk. Keep the horse very straight!

7 At B turn right, again as if you were riding a correct corner.

8 Upon reaching the track, "give" with the inside rein and pick up a trot with good impulsion.

9 Repeat the exercise in both directions, and also *without* changing direction—that is, making both the turn at E and B to the left, or both to the right.

10 Finally, ride the entire exercise in trot without the transitions to walk before the corners.

Turning Down the Centerline

Where You Go

Ride down the long side of the arena in working trot, tracking right. After the first corner of the short side, ride a transition to walk. At A or C, turn down the centerline. Pick up a trot and ride straight on the centerline, tracking left when you reach the far end. Repeat the exercise in both directions.

Why You Do It

For young horses and inexperienced riders, it is acceptable at first to maintain the bend found in the first corner of the short side and ride onto the centerline as part of a continuously curved line. However, as you progress in practice, it must be remembered that the short side is a straight line, and technically, the horse should be straightened after the first corner, making a clear new turn just before A or C to go down the centerline. As the horse's level of training increases, he should be able to make the turn closer and closer to A or C.

As in Exercises 1 and 2 (pp. 28 and 30), this exercise combines a walk transition with a turn. Due to the collecting effect of the downward transition, the rider has the chance to ride a more accurate turn. The transition to walk also allows the rider more time to prepare for the turn, to ride the turn, and to properly straighten the horse afterward for a correct upward transition. This exercise teaches the rider to use the outside rein to limit the size of the turn. It also prepares riders who wish to compete for a dressage test, as it asks them to ride a correct entry and centerline. Ride your centerline like I describe in this exercise, combine it with a proper salute, and

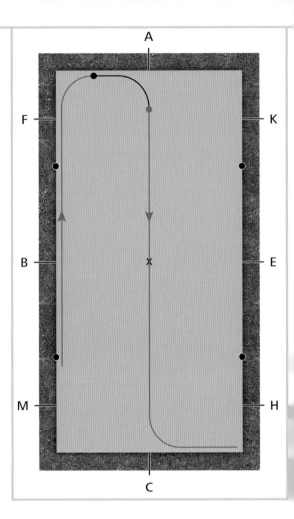

you've made an optimal first impression in the show ring!

Here's How

1 Trot down the long side of the arena, tracking right.
2 Use a half-halt to balance your horse as you approach the first corner of the short side.
3 After riding a *correct corner* (see Exercise 1, p. 28), use an additional half-halt to decrease the horse's tempo.
4 "Give" briefly on the reins to improve and test the horse's self-carriage.
5 Immediately after the "give," half-halt to a walk transition. "Package" your

horse by equally weighting both of your seat bones, closing both legs at the girth, and "taking" on both reins. If the horse slows too much or seems to want to stop, immediately "give" your hands forward to encourage him to stay "forward" in his movement.

6   As you approach the middle of the short side at A or C, ride your turn down the centerline. Bring your inside hip forward and your inside shoulder back. Your inside leg should be at the girth to send your horse forward while your outside leg stays a hand's width behind the girth to prevent the horse's haunches from swinging out during the turn and to help limit the size of the turn. The inside rein invites the horse to flex to the inside, while the outside rein allows for this and also prevents the horse's outside shoulder from bulging out).

7   As soon as you are on the centerline and facing A or C on the opposite short side, drive the horse straight forward with both seat bones and both legs. At the same time, give on the right rein and if needed, take more firmly on the left rein to insure that the horse's neck straightens after the turn.

8   This moment of straightening the horse is also the perfect time to ride the transition back to trot, using a quick aid with both calves, moderately weighting both seat bones, and briefly softening both reins.

9   Fix your gaze on a point straight ahead of you at the end of the centerline. If your horse "wiggles" as you move down the line, do not try to correct him with your reins. Instead, ride forward with good impulsion to help improve your horse's balance.

10 Use a half-halt to prepare for the left turn at the end of the centerline at A or C. Make your turn the same as you did in Step 6, but this time do it in trot. And, don't forget to ride correctly through the next corner as you move from the short side to the long side!

Having Problems?

- *Your horse "wavers" or "wiggles" from side to side, or drifts sideways on the centerline*. This is usually due to a general lack of impulsion. Ride energetically forward out of the turn onto the centerline! This will activate your horse's hind legs. If possible, have a friend on the ground watch you travel down the centerline to see if you collapse to one side with your body, which may mean you are inadvertently weighting one seat bone more than the other.

- *You overshoot the centerline and end up steering back toward it after your turn*. You need to turn earlier! Experiment with how far in advance you need to make your turn in order to hit the centerline accurately, and choose a "marker" to help you remember the starting point for the next attempt.

- *You and your horse become disorganized and lose the rhythm after the turn*. Did you prepare your horse adequately with a half-halt before the turn, or did you catch him by surprise with a sudden change of direction? If you don't give your horse any warning before you change your path of travel, it will take him longer to adjust his body. Too much inside flexion can also cause the horse to lose his rhythm.

Circles

I am constantly reminded how difficult it is to ride a correct circle. Many riders don't even realize that the figure they are riding is *anything* but round! Some ride deeply into the arena corners when riding a 20-meter circle (as if they are riding around the whole ring rather than a specific figure); others make their circles too small or too large. Some bulge out or fall in on the "open" side of the circle (the side that isn't along the wall or fence), or neglect to hit the track where they should at the *circle points* (see p. 20).

Riding a circle correctly requires maintaining a consistent degree of lateral bend in the horse. To achieve this, the rider must not only give the aids correctly, she must also focus on riding a *painfully* accurate path of travel. For example, on a 20-meter circle that begins at A or C, the horse will touch the track at three points: the starting point of A or C, and the two circle points, located on each long side, 10 meters from each corner. In a 20-meter by 40-meter arena, the circle will also touch X.

To do this the rider establishes the circle in the middle of one of the short sides of the arena. As soon as the horse reaches A or C, the rider begins steering him toward the first circle point on the track. Upon reaching the circle point, the rider steers toward X, from X she steers toward the next circle point on the opposite track, and from that circle point she completes the circle by returning to A or C.

Correct Circles

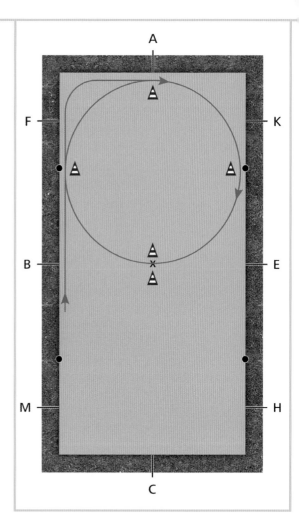

Where You Go

You need five cones or "markers" for this exercise. Place a cone at each point of a 20-meter circle: one just off the track at C or A (so you have room to ride between the cone and the arena fence or wall, one at each circle point (again, slightly inside the track), and then one on either side of X (in a small arena) so the path of your 20-meter circle goes between them.

Ride along the long side of the arena at the trot, tracking right. When you reach A on the short side, flex your horse to the right and steer him toward the next circle point. You will be guiding him slightly off the track in a curved line. As soon as your horse arrives at the circle point, steer him toward X. At X, pass between the two cones and then steer toward the next circle point. Even when you have reached the "safety net" of the track after traveling along the open side of the circle, remember that the remaining quarter of the circle must still be ridden as a *curved line* until A is reached again. At A the 20-meter circle is completed, and you can proceed around the arena on the track.

Why You Do It

Being able to ride an exact circle line is of crucial importance. Placing cones or markers around the points of the circle make the correct line easier for the rider to visually identify and ride accurately. Riding through each "gate" formed by the cones and the fence line teaches the rider to recognize the aids necessary to keep the horse on a consistently round circle. The cones make it harder for the rider to "cheat" by flattening out the open side of the circle.

Here's How

1   As you trot through the first corner onto the short side of the arena and approach A (the start of your 20-meter circle), bring your inside hip forward and drive with your inside leg at the girth to establish lateral bend and encourage the horse to step under his body with his inside hind leg.

2   Apply a "guarding" outside leg to help keep the horse's outside hind leg active. When combined with the outside rein, your outside leg also prevents the horse from drifting out. The outside rein needs

to allow for a slight inside flexion of a degree relative to the arc of the circle.

3 Use half-halts at regular intervals to keep your horse "packaged" and balanced as you guide your horse onto the path of the circle, using the seat and leg aids described above and a slight opening inside rein.

4 As soon as your horse responds with the appropriate lateral bend, soften the inside rein while keeping your horse thinking "forward."

5 When you reach the next circle point, ride the continuing turn in the same manner—your goal is to achieve a *round* circle!

6 After passing through the "gate" at X and heading back toward the track, you will need to ride with increased outside aids to prevent your horse from falling out, and as a result, reaching the track *before* the circle point.

7 Ride the final quarter of the circle (back to A) just as you did the first three.

8 Repeat for several circles, then change directions.

Having Problems?

• *Your horse constantly drifts outward on the circle.* You may be asking him for too much lateral bend in his neck toward the inside. Keep him straighter so that you only see his inside eye and the edge of his inside nostril. For the time being, use very clear seat and leg aids. A horse that is strung out and unbalanced may also drift outward. Use half-halts to organize, activate, and "package" him.

• *Your horse constantly falls in on the circle.* This usually means your horse is not fully accepting your inside leg and is avoiding bending laterally. Work with your horse so that he easily "gives" in his

neck when you ask him to flex inward. Drive your horse forward while repeatedly—but briefly—applying your inside rein aid to attain flexion, and then immediately "giving" the rein when he responds. If the horse is too strong in the trot, try riding the circle in walk. Once you can easily flex your horse to the inside, he will better accept your inside leg and allow himself to bend laterally—which means you will better negotiate the path of the circle.

Riding a Square

Where You Go

Exercise 5 should be attempted only once you have practiced Exercises 1 through 4. Keep in mind the progression of the previous exercises as you ride a square within a 20-meter circle: Begin a corner at A, then ride a straight line to the circle point on the rail, where you ride another corner onto another straight line to X. At X, ride another corner, heading to the circle point on the opposite track, where your final corner sends you back to A. This exercise can be ridden in all gaits.

Why You Do It

This exercise helps correct the horse that "falls through" his outside shoulder (on the *outside* of the square). This means the horse's weight falls to that shoulder—a problem that is usually caused either by the rider's inadequate use of the outside rein or the horse's inadequate response to it. Because this exercise calls for riding straight lines *without* inside flexion, it clarifies the value of the outside rein for both horse and rider. The horse that tends to carry more weight on his outside foreleg will begin to bear weight more evenly on his legs after *Riding a Square*.

Here's How

1 After riding down the track and coming onto the short side traveling in either direction, turn at A while keeping the next circle point (on the rail) in view. Make this turn by pushing your inside hip (the one closest to the center of the square) forward, drive with your inside leg at the girth, and keep your outside leg in the guarding position, just behind the girth. Your outside rein should allow your in-

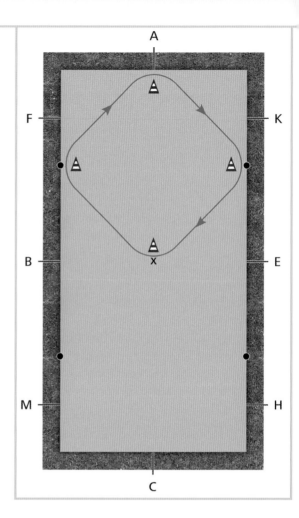

side rein to ask the horse to flex and turn.

2 As soon as your horse leaves the track at A to travel to the first circle point, ride him in a straight line: Both seat bones equally weighted, both legs at the girth driving the horse forward, and the horse's neck straight between both reins. A strong half-halt on the outside rein may be necessary to achieve the desired straightness.

3 Ride a half-halt as you go into the "corner" of the square at the circle point and then continue, riding to X and making the turn onto the next straight line as described above.

4 Practice this exercise in both directions.

"Stretchy" Canter Spirals

Where You Go

Ride on a circle at the canter. Reduce the size of the circle by spiraling inward until you have reached the size of a volte, all the while maintaining the impulsion in a forward canter. Stay on the small volte for two or three energetic rounds, then begin to incrementally increase the size of your circle while letting the horse stretch forward and downward on a longer rein.

Why You Do It

This is a nice exercise at the end of the horse's warm-up or after a long session in collected canter. As the horse spirals inward in a forward canter, he must truly use his inside hind leg, lower his inside hip, and shift his weight back onto his haunches in order to stay on the required circle line. Letting the horse stretch as you spiral back out tests whether the horse has successfully worked "over the back" and used his whole body in the exercise.

Here's How

1 Pick up the canter on a circle: Your inside seat bone (inside the bend) should be weighted; your inside leg at the girth to maintain impulsion; your outside leg behind the girth to prevent the hindquarters from falling out; and your outside rein should prevent the horse's outside shoulder from bulging out (see p. 13). Your inside rein controls the amount of flexion toward the inside.

2 Use the inside rein to guide your horse little by little toward a volte at the circle's center. Make sure to "give" the inside rein frequently to allow the horse's

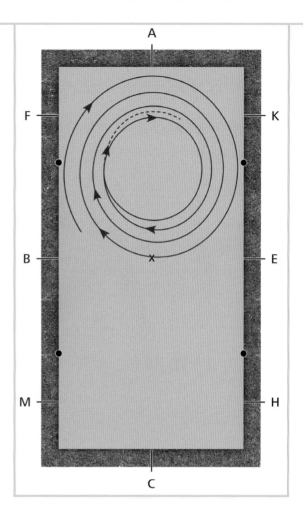

inside hind leg to step under his body. Even as you spiral in on a smaller circle, *do not* shorten your horse's canter strides!

3 Use your outside aids to prevent your horse from drifting out as you spiral in.

4 Decrease the circle as much as you can while still giving and taking on the inside rein. In other words, you should not have the feeling that you must hold constantly on the inside rein to keep the horse spiraling in.

5 Once you reach a circle the size of a volte, ride two to four of them before then beginning to spiral out onto larger circles.

6 As you gradually enlarge the circle size,

Here you see very nice stretching forward and downward as the canter circle increases.

let the horse stretch forward and downward on a longer rein.

7 While still encouraging the horse to stretch on a long rein, ride a transition to trot and then down to walk.

8 Give the horse a short break and then repeat the exercise in the other direction.

Having Problems?

- *You have great difficulty spiraling inward.* You may be sending the horse mixed signals by pushing your inside seat bone *outward* when you weight it. Or perhaps you are collapsing in your inside hip. Concentrate on lengthening your legs down and stretching straight up out of your hips with your upper body. When riding a particularly sensitive horse, make sure he does not bring his haunches in as you decrease the circle size. Be sure that your "end volte" is a size that is appropriate for your horse's level of training.

- *Your horse isn't reaching forward into the contact and stretching as you increase the circle size.* This issue is often the result of a canter that is flat and a lack of "swing" over the horse's back as you spiral inward. Fix a lack of stretching in the second part of this exercise (the spiral out) by maintaining more activity and "jump" in the canter in the first part (the spiral in).

Lengthening and Shortening the Canter on a Circle

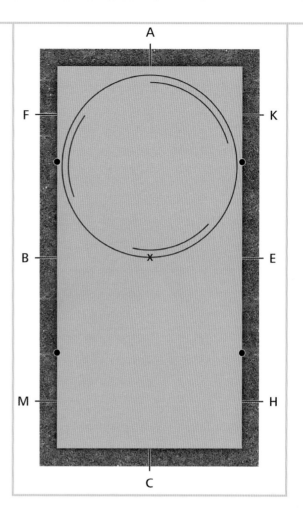

Where You Go

Canter on a circle. Ride six canter strides at a more forward pace, then shorten the horse's stride for the next six. Ride the next six strides more forward again, and then shorten again.

Why You Do It

This exercise improves the horse's response to the forward-driving aids in the canter, creates an opportunity to school the horse in changes of pace, and when ridden correctly, teaches the horse not to swing in or out with his hindquarters during transitions within the gait. Additionally, the inward flexion required on the circle helps improve the horse's connection during such transitions: Going more forward and then shortening stride and then going more forward again activates the hindquarters and optimizes the level of "throughness."

Here's How

1 Ride a *correct circle* using the standard aids (see p. 36). Use many half-halts to keep your horse's canter active and "through," and test your horse's self-carriage by frequently "softening" your hands.

2 Lengthen the horse's stride using quick, impulse-like forward-driving aids. Your inside rein must allow the resulting increased energy to be released *forward*.

3 Count out six canter strides.

4 Then shorten the horse's stride by "catching" the push from his hindquarters achieved in the forward phase of the exercise. Do this by using many small giving and taking rein aids and sitting deeply in the saddle.

5 Again count out six canter strides.

6 Ride forward again, and so on. Gradually work toward leaving the circle and riding the exercise using the whole ring.

7 Practice in both directions.

Having Problems?

• *Your horse comes off the aids, or becomes flat and hurried, when you push him forward.* Use more half-halts, and if needed, use a stronger aid once to change the horse's pace (shorten his

Adele is moving freely forward in working canter on the closed side of a circle.

stride) more clearly early in the exercise to keep his hind legs underneath him. Don't overwhelm him in the "forward phase" by asking for too much lengthening of stride right away. Increase the length of stride gradually.

- *Your horse won't let you bring him back after the lengthening.* If you rode forward too ambitiously and "crossed the line," going beyond the point where you could maintain control of your horse, now you may have a problem! Your horse may have tensed up his muscles to a degree that he is no longer able to "hear" your aids. It might seem as though the only way to get him back under control is by applying strong use of the reins. Instead, use an opening inside rein to guide his forehand

slightly inward and keep enough inside leg on to hold his haunches out. Imagine that you want your horse to leg-yield off your inside leg. This isn't truly possible in the canter in the way that it is in walk and trot, but by using the same aids, the horse will "give" in his neck and poll toward the inside of the circle while maintaining active hindquarters. This "loosening" of the neck and poll will enable him to respond to your half-halts, and other signals. In general, you can prevent the horse from becoming too strong by carefully increasing the amount of "forward" and lengthening in small increments: Only ask for more when the horse can stay on the aids at the pace you previously requested.

Leg-Yield-to-Straight on the Circle

Where You Go

On the right rein, ride in walk on a circle just to the inside of the track. When you reach the open side of the circle ask your horse to leg-yield his haunches away from your right leg. After a few sideways steps, ask your horse to go straight forward along the curved path of the circle again. Then, as you approach the closed side of the circle, ask the horse to leg-yield again. Continue alternating between leg-yield and traveling straight along the path of the circle several times around.

Why You Do It

By alternating between moving sideways and moving straight ahead, your horse will become more supple. This exercise improves flexibility in the horse's poll, neck, and hindquarters. The inside flexion required in the leg-yield will improve the horse's flexion on the circle, and the constant change of positioning will teach the horse to react promptly to the aids (he will become more "through"). The rider's coordination and the timing of her aids will also improve as she strives to ride the exercise with fluid transitions between the phases of straight and sideways movement.

Here's How

1 Begin on the right rein, riding a circle in walk, slightly to the inside of the track.
2 Upon reaching the open side of the circle, prepare to leg-yield your horse's haunches to the outside of the circle. Use an opening inside rein to guide your

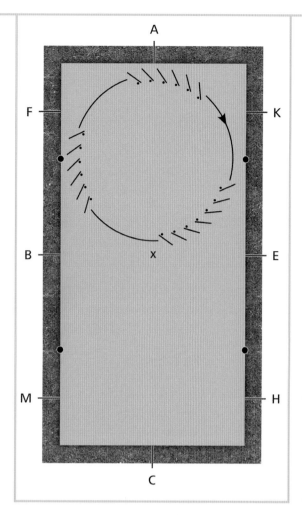

horse's forehand inward, as if you want to ride toward the middle of the circle.
3 Once your horse is positioned inward, bring your right (inside) leg slightly back, weight your inside seat bone and drive the horse sideways to the left.
4 The outside rein helps guide the horse sideways to the left and ensures that he doesn't overbend to the right.
5 Your left (outside) "guarding" leg prevents the haunches from coming out too far, which would cause the horse to move too much to the side and not enough forward.
6 The inside rein should "give" as frequently as possible to allow the horse's

inside hind leg to cross over his outside hind leg.

7 Each rein must continuously work in conjunction with the other: The inside rein guides the forehand inward to create sideways movement, and then lightens to allow the outside rein to keep the horse on the (circular) path of travel. Then, before the inside flexion diminishes, the inside rein comes into play again to maintain it.

8 After several steps of leg-yield, let your horse glide seamlessly back to tracking straight ahead on the circle. Your inside leg returns to driving at the girth; your inside seat bone stops driving sideways; your inside hip is positioned only slightly forward, and your outside aids prevent the horse from drifting outward onto the track.

9 After a few steps straight, ask your horse to leg-yield again off your inside leg.

10 Ride this exercise for a few circles and then repeat in the other direction and at the trot.

Having Problems?

- *It requires a lot of effort on your part to ride the transition to the leg-yield.* As always, several half-halts are necessary to prepare for the leg-yield on the circle. If you hang too long on the inside rein after half-halting you will hinder the fluidity of the horse's movement. Of course, it is also more challenging for the horse to move sideways than straight ahead. After a few repetitions of the exercise, the horse should more willingly respond to your sideways-driving aids. If not, you can try riding the leg-yield "more clearly" by asking the horse for more sideways angle and a greater degree of crossing of his legs. It is harder for the horse to "weasel out" of the leg-yield when he is more clearly positioned to the side.

- *Your horse loses rhythm and forwardness when asked for the leg-yield.* In this case, you may be asking for more angle (of his body on the circle) than the horse can accommodate while maintaining fluid movement. If this is happening, think "less is more!" A constant "holding" inside rein aid can also block the horse from moving forward with regularity. Frequently soften the inside rein, even if only for a brief moment! Be willing to take a good look at your riding and consider what you may be doing to cause the problem—and then work to correct it.

- *You are unsure about how to move your horse sideways and forward at the same time.* Steer the horse's head and forehand toward the middle of your circle, as if you want to ride right into the middle of it. This guides his forehand onto the track of a slightly smaller circle while his haunches remain on the track of your original circle. In the moment in which your horse would actually step toward the middle of the circle if you let him, use the aids for leg-yielding (see p. 43) to cause him to step sideways and forward instead of just forward. Use your outside rein more during the leg-yield than when you first guide the horse's forehand inward toward the center of the circle.

- *The exercise goes well in walk but not so well in trot.* Wait, and do not attempt to ride this exercise in trot until you can shorten the horse's stride in trot while softening the reins without the horse running forward (see Exercise 7, p. 41). If you attempt this before you and your horse are ready, the horse may try to lean on your hands and avoid activating his hind legs.

Walk-Trot Transitions while Leg-Yielding

Where You Go

Ride on a circle just to the inside of the track in trot, tracking right. Shorten the horse's stride and ask him to leg-yield on the circle, with his forehand pointed toward the middle of the circle (see Exercise 8, p. 43). While leg-yielding, use half-halts to ride a transition to walk. Continue asking the horse to leg-yield on the circle in walk for several strides. Then, while still leg-yielding, ride a transition back to trot. Slightly decrease the horse's sideways angle while riding the upward transition. Once the trot is established, ride your horse straight ahead on the circle—find a forward, working trot with good impulsion. Then repeat the exercise.

Why You Do It

Riding transitions as the horse steps sideways is beneficial for activating his inside hind leg. This exercise also improves the horse's musculature around his ribs and abdomen, thereby increasing the horse's flexibility. The inside flexion required when working on a circle keeps the horse supple at the poll. The connection of the horse's back end through his front end during the transitions becomes more stable.

Here's How

1 Trot on a circle, just inside the track, on the right rein.
2 Shorten the stride in trot by driving the horse into a briefly "holding" hand (see p. 13).
3 Guide the horse's forehand slightly toward the middle of the circle with your

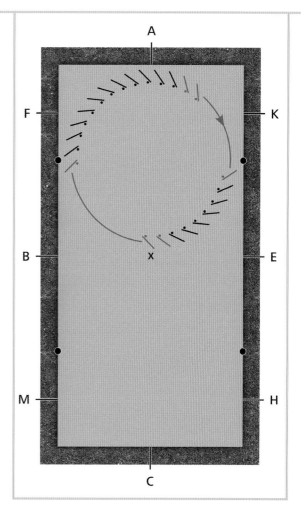

right rein while using your weighted inside seat bone and sideways-driving inside leg to send the horse's haunches *out*.

4 When the horse is leg-yielding obediently and maintaining a correct connection from back to front, ride a transition to walk: Continue to give the aids for leg-yield, but sit deeper and half-halt by giving and taking on the reins, somewhat strongly if needed, to bring the horse down to the walk.

5 Immediately soften the inside rein once your horse is walking.

6 Continue riding leg-yield on the circle for several strides.

7 Now, return to the trot while maintaining the leg-yield. Use a stronger inside leg aid while giving and taking on the inside rein.

8 Decrease the angle of the leg-yield until you are eventually riding straight on the circle: Guide the forehand outward with the left rein and bring the haunches back in with your left leg positioned slightly behind the girth.

9 Ride a nice forward trot, traveling straight ahead on the circle for a ways before repeating the exercise.

10 Practice in both directions.

Having Problems?

- *Your horse comes above the bit as you begin the leg-yield*. You must become more accurate in the timing of your rein aids. Aim to half-halt for a shorter duration but more frequently on the inside rein. The outside rein actually maintains a steady contact and is responsible for the horse's frame. The outside rein should only be momentarily softened when the forehand moves inward as the horse is initially positioned on an angle in preparation for the leg-yield.

- *Your horse won't pick up the trot while leg-yielding in walk*. You may be pressing your inside leg against your horse with unchanging pressure in an attempt to maintain the angle on the circle as you leg-yield. Focus on using short, pulse-like aids. Use a quick leg aid, then relax your leg and wait to see if your horse responds. Only repeat the leg aid if it is truly necessary. This is the way to keep your horse "in front of the leg," meaning he responds to *light* leg aids. If the horse is in front of the leg, he will trot when asked with a *stronger* leg aid, even during the leg-yield.

Spiraling In and Out while Leg-Yielding

Where You Go

Track right on a 20-meter circle in trot. Spiral inward, riding smaller and smaller circles, until you are riding a volte. Then spiral outward on larger and larger circles by leg-yielding your horse off your right leg. Upon arriving back on the path of a 20-meter circle, straighten your horse so that he is only bent to the proper degree to accommodate the curved line of travel.

Why You Do It

Spiraling out on the circle in leg-yield improves flexibility in the horse's poll and encourages the horse to step actively underneath his body with his inside hind leg. This improves the horse's "pushing power" and sends him into the outside rein.

Here's How

1 Track right in trot on a 20-meter circle. Your inside (right) hip should be forward, your inside leg driving at the girth, and your outside (left) leg in the "guarding" position. The inside rein is responsible for establishing flexion to the inside, which is allowed but also (appropriately) limited by the outside rein.

2 To begin the spiral in, guide the horse progressively in toward the center of the circle with your inside rein while keeping him trotting actively forward with your inside leg at the girth. Your outside aids should prevent the horse from drift back outward.

3 Once you have reached the volte in the middle (the smallest possible circle

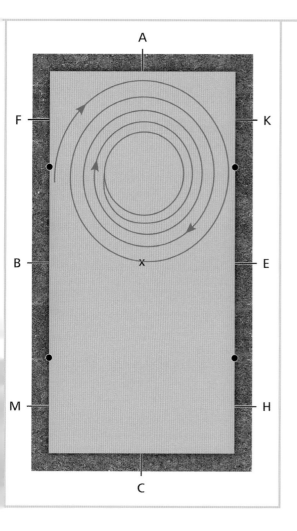

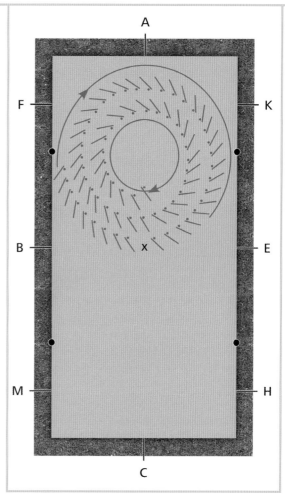

at your horse's level of training), ride around it one or two times while sending the horse from your inside leg into the outside rein. Shorten his trot stride using half-halts.

4 Next move your inside (right) leg back slightly and use it, along with your inside seat bone, to drive the horse's hindquarters sideways (left). Ask momentarily for more flexion with the inside rein.

5 Once the horse is positioned at a slight angle relative to the curved line of travel, give slightly on the inside rein to allow the horse's hind legs to cross over.

6 Use the outside rein to guide the horse outward in the moment in which the inside rein gives, gradually increasing the size of the circle.

7 The aids for the leg-yield left should be given repeatedly, along with the aids used to guide the horse out onto a progressively larger circle, so that the horse does not straighten.

8 Upon reaching the track of the 20-meter circle again, use the outside rein to bring your horse's forehand in line with his haunches. Return your inside leg to the girth and drive the horse straight forward on the circle in a swinging trot with good impulsion.

9 Change directions and try the exercise tracking left.

Having Problems?

- *The exercise seems too challenging for you and your horse.* Try riding it at the walk first. Then as a next step, try spiraling inward in trot, ride a transition to walk, and leg-yield back out to the 20-meter circle in the walk.

- *Your horse does not truly move sideways while spiraling out.* Position your horse at a steeper angle than is actually necessary for the leg-yield, relative to the path of travel. If the horse then starts crossing his legs correctly (moving *sideways* as well as *forward*), diminish the amount of angle. Also make sure the horse is staying straight within his body. If there is too little outside rein contact the horse will fall out through his outside shoulder and evade crossing his legs.

Additional Challenge

Shoulder-in can be developed out of this exercise once the horse willingly leg-yields out on the circle. Increase the use of your outside leg, change the aid given by the inside seat bone (you don't send the horse so much sideways in shoulder-in), and create more lateral bend. Using half-halts—driving the horse from the inside leg to the outside rein—helps the horse achieve an increasingly uphill balance.

Canter Transitions Out of Leg-Yield

Where You Go

Tracking left, on a 20-meter circle, at the walk. On the open side of the circle, leg-yield your horse off your left leg (moving his haunches out to the right), and when you reach the closed side of the circle, ride a transition to canter. Canter one or one-and-a-half times around the circle, then transition back to a walk. Repeat the exercise.

Why You Do It

Leg-yielding on the circle encourages the horse to step further under his body with his inside hind leg. This improves the horse's connection with the outside rein, as well as his inside flexion, allowing the rider to be softer on the inside rein. These are important criteria when aiming for a good transition to canter. You will notice how similar the aids for the leg-yield are to the aids for the canter.

Here's How

1 Walk on the left rein, beginning a 20-meter circle at one end of the arena.
2 When you reach the open side of the circle, use your left rein to guide the horse's forehand inward, toward the middle of the circle.
3 Once the horse is positioned at the desired angle relative to the direction of travel (a maximum of 45 degrees) weight your inside (left) seat bone, place your inside leg behind the girth to drive the horse forward and sideways, and place your outside (right) leg in the guarding position.

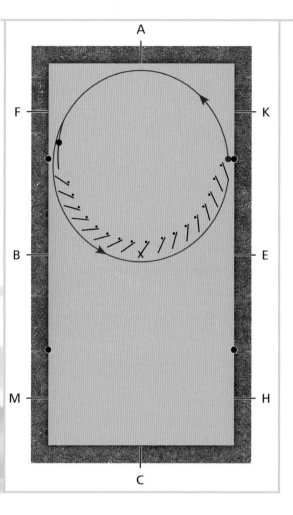

4 The outside rein keeps the horse on the path of the circle. The inside rein gives and takes, and it is responsible for maintaining a consistent degree of inside flexion.

5 When you reach the circle point on the track after leg-yielding around the entire open side of the circle, use your outside rein to limit the horse's sideways movement, push your inside hip more forward, and return your inside leg to the girth while the outside leg stays back in the guarding position.

6 The canter transition should naturally occur just with the use of a preparatory half-halt, your inside hip moving forward with increased weight, and the

These three photos show the first steps of the leg-yield on the open side of the circle.

inside rein "softening" to allow for the first stride of canter.

7   Your inside leg at the girth helps keep the canter forward and active.

8   Collect the canter using many half-halts, and then ride the transition to walk. If you and your horse cannot yet ride a transition from canter to walk, then substitute a downward transition to trot and then to walk.

9   Repeat this exercise several times in both directions.

Having Problems?

- *Your horse comes off the aids in the canter*. Use predominantly your outside rein and less inside rein to keep the horse "through," so you can "soften" the inside rein in the moment of the canter depart to allow the horse to take the first canter stride. After a few attempts your horse will be better able to maintain the connection during the transition. Also make sure that your horse reacts immediately to your forward-driving aid. Don't let him delay as it will impede the effectiveness of your aids and make for a less fluid transition.

- *Your horse responds poorly to the canter aid*. You may be letting the "positive tension" you built up during the leg-yield disappear prior to the transition, rather than using it. Keep your focus after the leg-yield—only when the horse is in a well established canter should you "just sit there" for a moment and let the horse carry you along.

Walk-Canter Spirals

Where You Go

At the canter on the left rein, begin a 20-meter circle at one end of the arena. Briskly spiral in, decreasing the size of the circle while at the same time shortening the stride in canter. Once you are on a volte in the middle of the circle (the smallest size your horse can travel at his level of training), use half-halts to ride a transition to walk. Walk on the volte, organize your horse so that he is ready to give you a good canter transition, then canter from the walk, increasing the size of the circle while riding a fresh, forward tempo.

Why You Do It

Transitions from the canter to the walk, just like those from trot to walk, help collect the horse. Transitions out of the canter are often more difficult than those from the trot. It is easier to ride a canter-to-walk transition on a bending line (the spiraling circle) because the horse will begin to take more weight onto his haunches as he has to travel along the path of smaller and smaller circles. On the smaller circles, the horse stays naturally more collected, which leads to a better upward transition back to the canter. Prior to that, the walk phase on the volte provides the rider an opportunity to reorganize before spiraling back out—for example, you can reestablish rein contact if it was lost. By riding many correct canter-walk transitions, the horse's carrying capacity, ability to collect, and "throughness" improves. In addition, the rider who practices many transitions like this gains a fine-tuned sense of the aids, and is well on her way to making her aids "invisible!"

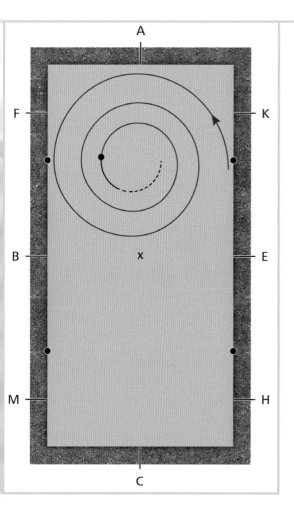

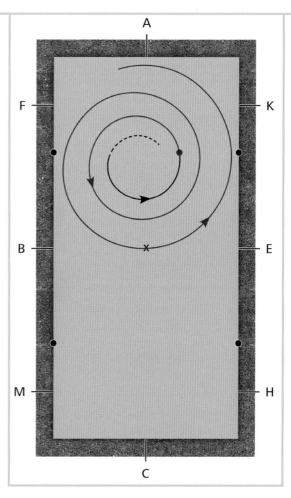

Here's How

1 Canter on a 20-meter circle tracking left. Your inside (left) hip should be forward, your inside leg driving at the girth, and your outside (right) leg placed behind the girth to prevent the horse's haunches from falling out. The outside rein limits the amount of inside flexion and prevents the horse from "bulging out" with his outside shoulder, while the inside rein is responsible for maintaining an appropriate degree of flexion.

2 Use your inside rein to guide the horse inward onto progressively smaller-sized circles. As in previous exercises (see pp. 39 and 46) the horse should travel inward on a spiral-shaped path, but this time he should arrive at the middle volte more quickly than in previous exercises—one or two times round should be all it takes to reach the volte in the circle's center.

3 Use your outside aids to keep your horse straight while spiraling inward. Too much inside flexion is detrimental to this exercise because it prevents the horse's hind legs from stepping well under his center of gravity, meaning he cannot rock weight back onto his haunches in the canter. The downward transition to the walk will then only be possible with heavy use of the reins, resulting in the horse coming onto the forehand. This is *definitely not* what you want!

4 While spiraling in, use many half-halts to shorten the horse's canter stride. However, you should not be cantering more slowly: Keep the activity! Do this by driving your horse into a "holding" rein aid for one stride, then be passive for the next canter stride and "soften" your hand. In the next stride, half-halt to collect the horse, and then again be "quiet" with your aids for a stride—and so on.

5 If your horse is not accustomed to collecting his canter, do not ask for a long phase of collection or he will tire and may become disorganized or tense (either reaction is counterproductive for riding a good transition). When you can "soften" your hands, or at least the inside (left) hand, repeatedly, and your horse maintains his steady, collected pace, *don't wait*! Ask for the transition to walk right then and there.

6 Give a stronger version of the half-halts you used to shorten the horse's canter stride in Step 4 (think of riding an actual halt) to bring the horse to the walk. It is important that you do not constantly "hold" with your hands during the entire transition, but instead, give and take on the reins. Otherwise, your horse may harden against your hand or come above the bit.

7 If your horse becomes "dissatisfied" with the rein contact during the canter-walk transition, then as soon as he is in the walk, work to softly reestablish "throughness" so he is happy with the connection again before you proceed to the next step.

8 When you are ready to transition to canter, drive your horse from the inside leg into the outside rein. Then release the leg pressure and ask for the canter immediately by pushing your inside seat bone forward, giving on the inside rein, and moving your outside leg back.

9 Once cantering, increase the size of the circle just as quickly as you decreased it. Keep the inside flexion while spiraling outward. Don't forget to use your inside leg as well as the reins! Ride nicely forward in a big, working canter.

10 Repeat the exercise several times in each direction.

Having Problems?

- *Your horse falls out on the circle when you try to shorten his stride.* Use less inside rein. Keep your horse very straight. Imagine that you are sitting on a stiff, straight, wooden board, and you must steer it inward on the circle. Keep your horse's hind feet directly in line with his front feet, as if he is that wooden board. No part of the horse should "bulge out" of that straight line. Note that this correction should only be used temporarily, or it will detract from the connection from the back to the front of the horse. As soon as the horse better accepts the outside aids, flexion and bending should be reestablished.

- *Your horse trots several steps in the canter-walk transition.* Be patient. It usually takes several attempts to ride a successful transition. The rider also needs time to develop a feel for the duration and degree of collection necessary in preparation for the transition. If a small improvement is perceivable from transition to transition, then the horse and rider are on the right track.

20–15–10

Where You Go

Pick up a trot on the left rein and ride a 20-meter circle at one end of the arena. Ride once around the circle. Then, starting at the middle of the short side at A or C, ride a second, smaller circle 15 meters in diameter. Ride once around and finish with a 10-meter volte, which also begins and ends at A or C.

Why You Do It

This exercise increases the horse's lateral bend and helps improve carrying capacity. Each circle prepares the horse for the increased difficulty of the next, smaller circle. This exercise is especially well suited to young or green horses since it gradually introduces them to smaller and smaller circles rather than surprising them with a single small circle at a random point in the ring.

Here's How

1 Trot a 20-meter circle, tracking left, using the aids described in Exercise 4 (see p. 36).

2 When you reach the middle of the short side at A or C, begin a 15-meter circle. Prepare for the turn onto this smaller circle with a half-halt so that the horse steps further underneath his body with his hind legs. Use a firm inside (left) leg aid to maintain the impulsion. Your outside (right) guarding leg must come into play to ensure the horse's hind feet directly follow the tracks made by the front feet. Create inside flexion with the inside rein, but use enough outside rein to keep your horse from drifting out.

3 Use half-halts periodically to make sure the horse carries himself and doesn't lean on your hand.

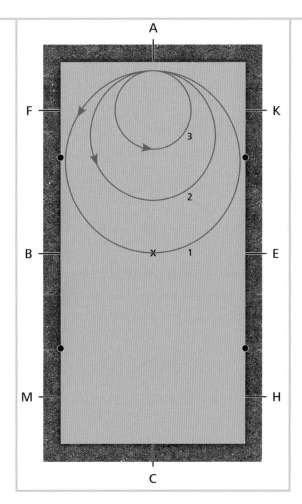

4 Once you have ended the 15-meter circle at A or C, ride seamlessly onto your 10-meter volte.

5 To begin the volte, use a somewhat stronger version of the aids described in Step 2 to guide the horse onto the smallest circle requiring the greatest degree of bend his training allows. If the horse willingly trots the volte without losing flexion, bend, rhythm, or impulsion, minimize your aids as much as possible. It is very important to keep only a light contact with the inside rein as much as possible!

6 Once you have ended your 10-meter volte at A or C, you have completed the exercise. Ride straight along the track

at a forward pace, change directions, and begin the exercise tracking the other way. This exercise can also be done in canter by the more advanced horse and rider.

Tip

If you aren't sure how large each size circle in the 20-15-10 exercises should be, consider using cones as markers as you did in Correct Circles (Exercise 4, p. 36). Measure your stride on the ground and match it to a meter, like many cross-country and jumping riders do. Then start at A or C and walk a straight line toward X, taking meter long steps as you go. When you reach 10 meters, place a cone, and when you reach 15 meters, place a cone, and finally, place one at X as your 20-meter marker. When using Exercise 13, ride your horse slightly to the inside of each cone on the corresponding circle. The marker will keep you honest in terms of the accuracy of your circles, and your horse will be less likely to "bulge out" with his outside shoulder and drift outward without you noticing.

Larger, Faster–Smaller, Slower

Where You Go

Ride a 20-meter circle on the right rein in working canter at one end of the arena. When you reach A or C, lengthen the stride in canter once around the circle. Before reaching A or C again, bring back the canter, showing a clear transition to a slower pace. When you reach A or C the next time, ride one smaller circle, about 12 meters in diameter, in collected canter. Then return to the 20-meter circle and repeat.

Why You Do It

Lengthening the stride in this exercise helps improve impulsion, and by riding more forward on a circle, the horse can learn to stay straight. The exercise as a whole provides a good opportunity to school transitions within the canter, and the smaller circle helps the horse begin to take increased weight on his hindquarters while shortening his stride. After a few repetitions, each part of the exercise helps prepare the horse for the next part: As the horse lengthens his stride in canter, he becomes better able to keep the activity and cadence when his stride is shortened. Then, after shortening his stride correctly, the horse can create increased impulsion and expression in the lengthening.

Here's How

1 Begin a 20-meter circle on the right rein in working canter at one end of the arena.
2 Prepare your horse for the exercise by half-halting. Do not let him lean on your hands!
3 At A or C, ask the horse to lengthen his canter stride: Drive increasingly with

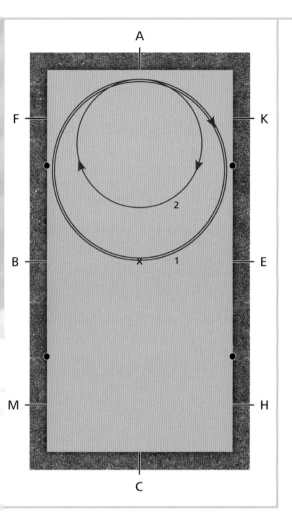

5 Shorten your horse's canter stride before reaching A or C again. Note that each horse will need a different amount of time to shorten his stride based on his level of "throughness." It may take a round or two for you to figure out how long your horse takes so that you can be accurate in your transition within the gait.

6 Continue to drive your horse forward, but contain the energy of the canter with brief, "holding" rein aids. These rein aids must always be followed by "giving" with the hands or problems with the contact will result.

7 When you reach A or C once more, turn onto the smaller 12-meter circle in what should now be a collected canter. The inside rein creates increased inside flexion, and the outside aids prevent the horse from drifting out. Maintain the activity in the canter!

8 Once completely around, return to the larger circle and lengthen the stride in canter. Repeat the exercise several times in each direction.

Having Problems?

- *Your horse stiffens and comes against the aids when you ask him to lengthen his stride.* Perhaps you are asking for too much lengthening, too soon. Begin with a very small, barely noticeable lengthening and gradually increase it as the horse remains connected and on the aids.

- *Your horse struggles to collect his canter and turn onto the smaller circle.* He's not ready for this exercise. Return to Exercises 7 and 12 for more practice changing pace (pp. 41 and 50).

your inside (right) seat bone and your inside leg positioned at the girth. "Let the bigger stride out" by softening both your hands. Keep the horse's hindquarters straight on the path of the circle with your outside (left) leg positioned behind the girth.

4 "Softening" your hands does *not* mean you should "throw the reins away" for the entire duration of the circle! The aids described in Step 3 should be given in the rhythm of the canter. The rider's inside leg, for instance, shouldn't squeeze constantly but should "breathe" with the horse as it is applied rhythmically.

Trotting Poles on the Circle

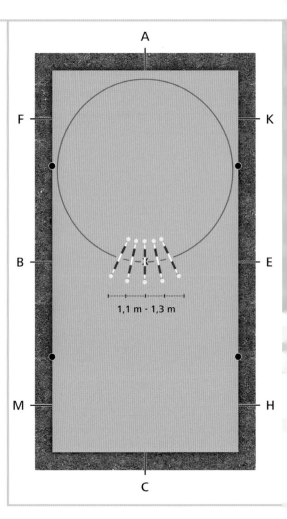

Where You Go

As shown in the diagram, lay out five trotting poles on the open side of a 20-meter circle. The length of your horse's trot stride determines the appropriate distance between cavalletti—it usually ranges from 3.5 to 4.25 feet (1.1 to 1.3 meters). Ride on the circle, and over the cavalletti, in trot.

Why You Do It

Cavalletti provide an excellent change of pace for the dressage horse. They help activate the horse's hind legs, strengthen his back and overall topline, and are an initial step toward introducing him to jumping, which is a useful skill and can lend interest to training. They also help improve the horse's coordination and provide the rider an opportunity to switch from the *dressage seat* to the *forward seat* (see p. 2).

Here's How

1 Begin on the closed side of your 20-meter circle in trot. You can choose rising or sitting trot for this exercise.

2 A few steps before reaching the cavalletti on the open side of the circle, change from your dressage seat to the forward

seat. As discussed at the beginning of this book, in the forward seat your base of support is comprised by your knees, calves, and heels (rather than your seat bones and the space between them, as in the dressage seat). Of course, when riding over cavalletti, only a moderate lightening of the seat is necessary: Keep your seat close to the saddle and just slightly close your hip angle.

3 As you approach the row of cavalletti, keep your horse between your leg and rein aids. Ride straight and forward on the curved line of the circle so that you set your horse up to go over the cavalletti successfully.

4 Upon reaching the cavalletti let the horse stretch his neck forward and down by moving your hands toward his mouth, but don't "throw away" the rein contact and be sure to maintain a balanced seat.

5 Your inside leg should send the horse forward the same degree as before the cavalletti—it shouldn't suddenly become stronger!

6 As you trot over the cavalletti, absorb the horse's increased reach and suspension in your legs and ankles so that you do not fall behind the motion.

7 Ride your 20-meter circle, going over the cavalletti, four or five times in a row, then repeat the exercise in the other direction.

Having Problems?

- *Your horse stops and refuses to go over the cavalletti or runs out to one side.* Begin the exercise approaching the cavalletti in the walk and only picking up a trot right before them. This gives you more control on the approach. Praise the horse when he goes over them! If the horse continues to try to run out to the side, lay a ground pole to the right and one to the left of the first cavalletti—at right angles to it—to help funnel him straight ahead.

- *Your horse drifts out while trotting over the cavalletti so that the distance between the last two is too large for his stride.* Use your "guarding" outside leg a bit more strongly to prevent your horse from "falling to the outside." Use your inside rein to help guide him inward. Your inside hand can open a little to the inside to help with this, but it should *not* pull backward!

Canter Cavalletti on the Middle Circle

Where You Go

As shown in the diagram on p. 58, place a single cavalletto on the centerline on each open side of a 20-meter circle at E or B (in the middle of the arena). For canter work, the cavalletti should be raised off the ground (if working with adjustable cavalletti, use them at their highest setting). If needed, ground poles set at right angles to each end of each cavalletto—as described in Exercise 15 (at left)—can help keep the horse straight in the approach and prevent run outs. Note the ground poles will need to be moved to the other side of the cavalletto when performing the exercise in the opposite direction.

Ride in forward seat (but remaining close to the saddle) the entire circle, passing over the two cavalletti each time around.

Why You Do It

This exercise is an opportunity for the rider to practice riding in the forward seat, and for those who cross-train, it serves as an introduction to jumping on a bending line. Canter cavalletti on the circle allow the rider to determine if her horse can stay on the aids, especially the outside aids, and they improve the horse's use of his back. The exercise also provides a nice change of pace for the horse and rider accustomed to schooling dressage figures regularly.

Here's How

1 Ride in canter tracking left and at B or E, begin a 20-meter circle in the middle of the arena. If you need to organize your-

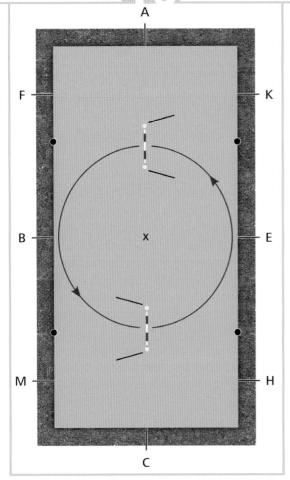

5 Then, "just wait" for the cavalletto to come as part of the circle and ride smoothly over it, hinging at your hips into the forward seat as you do. At the same time, your hands should "give" forward toward the horse's mouth, without throwing away the contact.

6 After the cavalletto, sit deep in the saddle to "package" your horse again before the next cavalletto.

Having Problems?

- *Your horse comes to a stop before the cavalletto and refuses to go over it.* Prepare your horse more thoroughly with trotting poles before trying canter cavalletti by returning to Exercise 15 (see p. 56). Then ride this exercise in trot. Use ground poles on each side of the cavalletti, as shown in the diagram, to help guide your horse over. Ride energetically forward! And remember, cavalletti are low enough, even at their highest setting, for a horse to step over them from a halt, if necessary, so even if the horse stops, don't allow him to turn right or left—drive him straight over.

- *Your horse drifts significantly to the outside after the cavalletto.* As you canter over the cavalletto, think of riding toward the inside of the 20-meter circle. Shift your weight to the inside and use your outside aids to prevent your horse from bulging out through his shoulder.

self or your horse in preparation for the exercise (or if you need to reestablish connection or organization at any time during the exercise), ride the circle as an oval so you go to the outside of the cavalletti.

2 Once you have your horse on the aids, steer him onto the true 20-meter circle in a place that allows enough time before the first canter cavalletto.

3 Keep your horse between your leg and rein aids. Find an energetic canter at a pace that is appropriate for your horse on the path of the circle.

4 Use half-halts as you approach the first cavalletto to get your horse's attention.

Turn-on-the-Forehand

Turn-on-the-forehand is a beneficial suppling exercise that is also very well suited to teaching horses to respond to the sideways-driving aids (see p. 10). Since the exercise can be performed slowly and can be broken down into small parts, even the inexperienced rider can get a feel for the timing and correct application of the aids during this exercise.

As the name implies, the horse comes to a halt and turns his hindquarters in a half-circle around his forehand, which remains more or less in the same place. The exercise should end with a square halt.

When riding this exercise in an indoor arena or a ring with a high fence, practice the movement inside the track so the horse has room for his head and neck.

A photo sequence showing the turn-on-the-forehand. It should begin and end with a calm, square halt.

Turn-on-the-Forehand on a Square

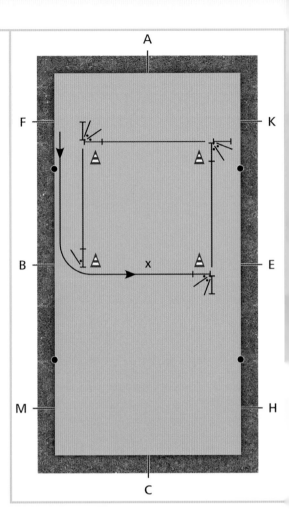

Where You Go

To prepare for this exercise, arrange four cones in a square in the arena (see diagram). At the walk, ride your horse along the outside of one side of the square shape that you have marked out. Halt in the "corner" of the square when *your* body (*not* the horse's head) is even with the cone. Ride a half-turn-on-the-forehand so that you turn 90 degrees and are facing the next side of the square. Then ride in walk toward the next cone, halt again, and ride another half-turn-on-the-forehand. Repeat all the way around the square.

Why You Do It

When beginning to learn the turn-on-the-forehand, it is easier to ride just a "half" correctly. This exercise is designed with multiple half-turns in succession. Since the exercise is ridden off the track, there isn't a wall or fence to act as a border, so the rider must practice using the outside aids or turn-on-the-forehand will become too big. As the horse crosses his hind legs over he becomes looser and more supple in the back. The turn-on-the-forehand also schools the horse to better respond to the sideways-driving leg aid. The transitions to halt and standing still improve obedience.

Here's How

1 Ride in walk around the square marked out by the cones. Each cone constitutes a corner. Once your horse is used to the cones and the path of the square, prepare to halt at an upcoming corner with a half-halt.

2 To halt when your body is even with the cone, contain your horse's forward movement with several giving and taking rein aids, weight both seat bones evenly, and have both calves at the girth.

3 When your horse has come to a halt, continue to sit tall in the saddle. This way your horse will maintain "positive" body tension.

4 Increase the weight on your inside (closer to the cone) seat bone and flex your horse to the inside.

5 The outside rein prevents the horse from over-flexing to the inside.

6 Move your inside leg slightly back to ask the horse to step sideways. The leg aid should continue to be applied in rhythm with the horse's steps. When the horse raises his inside hind leg, briefly soften the inside rein to allow the leg to step forward and sideways across the outside hind leg.

7 In the next moment the inside flexion should be reestablished with the inside rein. Both reins work together to prevent the horse from stepping forward with the forelegs.

8 Keep your outside leg slightly behind the girth in the "guarding" position to prevent the horse's hindquarters from stepping out too quickly.

9 To end the turn once facing straight down the new side of the square, ask the horse to halt again. Both your legs should be at the girth, both seat bones weighted equally, and your should have an equal feel on both reins.

10 Ride forward in a straight line until your body is across from the next cone, where you will repeat the half-turn-on-the-forehand.

11 Repeat the entire exercise several times in each direction until your horse responds easily to subtle aids.

Having Problems?

- *Instead of turning around the forehand, your horse overbends and "turns around his barrel."* This is a common mistake that is usually caused by riding with too much hand and not enough leg. The reins should only be used to prevent the horse from walking forward and to create a very slight amount of inside flexion to make it easier for the horse to respond to the sideways-driving leg.

- *Your horse ignores your sideways-driving aid and just moves forward.* Use both reins more clearly, especially as you start to ask for the turn. Use a stronger leg aid, reinforced with the spur or a tap with the whip on the same side, if necessary. Make sure you remember to increase the weight on your inside (closer to the cone) seat bone. Once your horse begins to respond correctly you can use lighter aids again.

- *Your horse steps backward in the turn.* This is the opposite problem as the one described above. Your horse is not sufficiently in front of the forward-driving aids. Perhaps you used too much hand to come to the halt at the cone. Try to use as little hand as possible and keep the horse energetically in front of the leg before halting. If your horse steps backward, immediately stop asking for the turn and ride forward a few steps before beginning the half-turn-on-the-forehand again.

Turn-on-the-Forehand with Cavalletti

Where You Go

To prepare for this exercise, place three or four cavalletti near the middle (between B and E) of the centerline, spaced at an appropriate distance for your horse's trot stride (usually about 4 feet or 1.20 meters). Turn onto the centerline in trot. Trot over the cavalletti and ride a transition to halt at the end of the centerline. Ride a full turn-on-the-forehand off your *right* leg (the horse's haunches move to the left). Trot back down the centerline, again going over the cavalletti and halting at the end, but this time ride a full turn-on-the-forehand off your *left* leg (the horse's haunches move to the right).

Why You Do It

In this exercise, horse and rider are required to complete several movements in quick succession: trotting over poles, a transition to halt and turn-on-the-forehand. The exercise improves the horse's coordination, response to the aids, and the activity of his hindquarters. Riding the turn-on-the-forehand without the support of the arena wall or fence tests whether the horse is truly responding to the rider's aids. Combining the different elements of this exercise help show how willingly your horse responds to your requests. The exercise also requires the rider to switch back and forth from a dressage seat to a forward seat over the cavalletti, which improves flexibility and security in the saddle.

Here's How

1   Turn onto the centerline in trot.

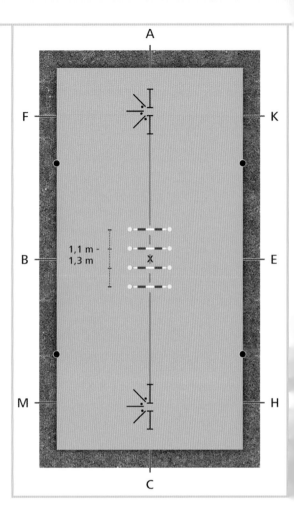

2   After turning, immediately straighten the horse and use half-halts to encourage him to step well underneath himself and "close" his frame.

3   Before the cavalletti, go into a forward seat but remain close to the saddle. Your weight should be supported by your knees, calves, and heels. *Do not* ride over the cavalletti in posting trot!

4   Keep your horse straight between your leg and rein aids so that he neither stops before the cavalletti nor runs out to the side.

5   Allow the horse to stretch his neck as he trots over the cavalletti by moving both hands forward. Make sure you do not fall behind the horse's motion.

6 After the cavalletti, return to a dressage seat and use half-halts to shift your horse into a more uphill balance again as you continue trotting down the centerline.

7 Prepare to halt your horse near the end of the centerline between F and K or M and H to ensure you have room to make the full turn-on-the-forehand. Weight both seat bones evenly, both legs should be at the girth, and both hands should give and take on the reins until the horse comes to a halt.

8 Once your horse is standing calmly, begin the first turn-on-the-forehand (off the right leg). Flex your horse to the right, move your right leg slightly back and increase the weight on your right seat bone to ask the horse to step with his hindquarters in a circle to the left around his forehand. Have your outside (left) leg ready to prevent the haunches from moving too quickly sideways if necessary, and to prevent the horse from turning more than the desired 180 degrees. The outside rein prevents the horse from over-flexing to the inside and works with the inside rein to prevent the horse from walking forward.

9 Once you have finished the full turn-on-the-forehand and are straight on the centerline but now facing the opposite direction, ride a transition to trot from the halt. Refocus the horse by briefly sitting more deeply in the saddle. Then use a quick leg aid to send your horse forward into the trot. Follow the horse's movement with your body and allow him to go forward with your hands.

10 Repeat the exercise in the same way as described in the previous steps, but this time ride the turn-on-the-forehand in the opposite direction—off the left leg.

11 Repeat the exercise several times in a row as well as later on during your schooling session.

Having Problems?

- Different kinds of problems can arrive in each of the three elements of this exercise: problems riding over cavalletti, coming to a halt, or with the turn-on-the-forehand. Therefore it is important to practice each element of the exercise by itself before you attempt stringing them together in such quick succession. The level of difficulty can also be decreased by riding the trot segment in walk, although be sure to space the cavalletti at an appropriate distance for the horse's walk stride (approximately 2.5 to 3 feet or 0.8 to 1 meter apart).

Cavalletti Tips

There are various ways to set up cavalletti depending on your intended goal:

1 Change the height of the cavalletti (raise them, or raise one side while the other side sits on the ground) to help improve the horse's coordination and attention.

2 Vary the number of poles to gain the horse's attention.

3 Change the distances between the poles to affect the horse's length of stride. A greater distance helps increase "pushing power" while a shorter distance increases cadence and carrying capacity.

Leg-Yielding

The leg-yield is a supling exercise and is commonly ridden at the walk. Once a rider has mastered the aids for leg-yield at the walk, she can also ask for it at the trot. The horse moves forward and sideways on two tracks while crossing his inside fore and hind legs over his outside legs. The horse is flexed at the poll (but not bent) away from the direction of travel. The horse should *not* be positioned at more than a 45-degree angle relative to the direction of travel.

The crossing over of the horse's legs loosens the muscles in his torso, which improves his overall relaxation and suppleness. Leg-yielding also improves the horse's response to the sideways-driving aids and stabilizes the contact with the outside rein. The leg-yield can be built into many different exercises to add variety to training.

Leg-Yield Inside-Outside

Where You Go

Walk around the arena just inside the track. At the beginning of a long side, ask your horse to leg-yield, off your inside leg. After a few successful steps, straighten him, and then ask him to leg-yield off your outside leg. After a few steps, straighten him again and leg-yield off the inside leg, and so on. Ride straight ahead on the short sides and use the long sides for *Leg-Yield Inside-Outside*. Repeat this exercise for several rounds around the ring in both directions. Keep each segment of leg-yield very short so that you frequently change the horse's flexion.

Why You Do It

This exercise is great for your warm-up. As the horse crosses his legs in the leg-yield, he becomes more supple. The change in flexion improves the suppleness in his poll, which in turn benefits the overall connection in his body from back to front. The coordination of the rider's aids and the horse's reaction to them will improve through the frequent change of positioning.

Here's How

1 Ride around the arena at the walk, aiming for *correct corners* on the short side and maintaining the inside flexion from the second corner as you ride onto the long side, just to the inside of the track.
2 Increase the weight on your inside (closest to center of the arena) seat bone.
3 Move your inside leg back behind the girth to send your horse forward and sideways. Don't exert constant pressure with your calf. Instead, use brief leg aids in rhythm with the horse's stride, ideally

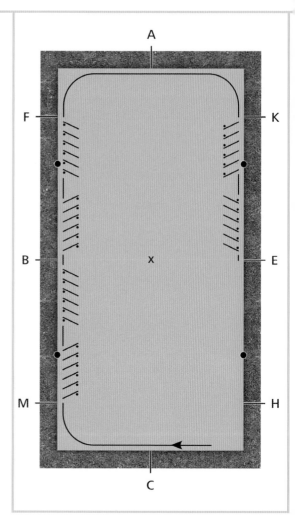

as he picks up his inside hind leg. Make sure to relax your leg again in between aids.

4 Your outside (closest to rail) leg should assume the "guarding" position behind the girth. Along with the inside leg, it is responsible for maintaining the horse's forward movement, but its main job is to prevent the horse's haunches from swinging too much to the outside.

5 The inside rein maintains the slight inside flexion. It is important to repeatedly give with the inside rein so as not to interrupt the flow of the horse's movement.

6 Maintain a steady contact with the outside rein. The outside rein should only be softened to the degree necessary to allow for the inside flexion.

7 After a few steps of leg-yield off the inside leg, straighten the horse again—use the outside rein to guide the forehand back in front of his haunches without flexing the horse to the outside.

8 As soon as your horse is straight between both your legs and reins, ask him to leg-yield off the outside leg, with his head positioned toward the track. Use your outside leg and seat bone in the same way described for yielding off the inside leg in previous steps.

9 After leg-yielding a few steps, straighten the horse again by bringing the forehand back in line with the haunches. As soon as the horse is straight, begin leg-yielding off the inside leg.

10 Continue the inside-outside pattern until you reach the end of the long side. Straighten the horse before turning onto the short side.

11 On the next long side begin the exercise again. Repeat in the other direction.

12 When this exercise is easy for you and your horse, try riding it in a slow trot. Only ask the horse for slight flexion at first.

Having Problems?

● *You can't achieve as many repetitions of leg-yield as depicted in the diagram.* In order to accomplish four inside-outside switches on one long side, your horse must respond immediately and willingly to subtle aids without requiring many corrections. This is something you must practice! Take as much time, or room, as you need. If you can only manage to change the flexion and direction of the leg-yield once, then aim to ride only the two sections of leg-yield on the long side. It is preferable to ride fewer repetitions correctly than to "pull" your horse back and forth because neither of you are prepared to do it correctly. Over time you will be able to flex your horse and direct him forward and sideways more efficiently. Then you will be able to end each leg-yield sooner, leaving more room to begin the next one.

A Nose-to-Rail Alternative

In my experience, leg-yielding nose-to-rail for long periods is not very motivating for the horse. Therefore, I recommend beginning with this inside-outside variation for both horse and rider. In the nose-to-rail leg-yield sections (off the leg closest to the rail) the wall or fence discourages the horse from evading the sideways-driving leg aid by running forward. This way, the rider can concentrate on coordinating seat, leg, and rein aids for the leg-yield without needing to use strong rein aids to prevent the horse from running off. Young horses also benefit from leg-yielding nose-to-rail initially—since less use of the reins is needed, the young horse can better maintain fluidity of movement while going sideways. The visual barrier of the wall or fence encourages the horse to move his haunches inward as the rider applies the sideways-driving aids. Switching to leg-yield off the inside leg (closest to the middle of the arena) tests the horse's understanding of the aids as he learns to do the exercise with his head pointing away from the wall.

Leg-Yield Across the Diagonal with a Volte

Where You Go

Ride in walk tracking right along the rail. At M or K, leg-yield across the diagonal off your left leg. At X, ride a 10-meter volte to the left. Then continue across the rest of the diagonal in leg-yield, straightening the horse when you reach the end of the long side. Note: In a 20 by 40 meter arena this exercise requires a fairly steep leg-yield. Riding this exercise in a 20 by 60 meter arena allows for a flatter leg-yield, which can also be ridden in a shortened trot stride. See p. 19 for more about arena sizes.

Why You Do It

This exercise shows whether your horse willingly follows your aids when you ask for him to move from the leg-yield across the diagonal, then straighten his body on a curved line (the volte), and finally return to the leg-yield. Switching from a movement that requires only flexion to one that also demands lateral bend necessitates different aids from the rider. This exercise improves the horse's suppleness, connection from back to front, and "throughness," while fine-tuning the rider's aids.

Here's How

1 Ride in walk tracking right down the long side of the arena. After the second corner on the short side (at M or K), ask your horse to leg-yield across the diagonal off your left leg: Increase the weight on your left seat bone, use your left leg behind the girth to send the horse forward-and-sideways, and flex the horse

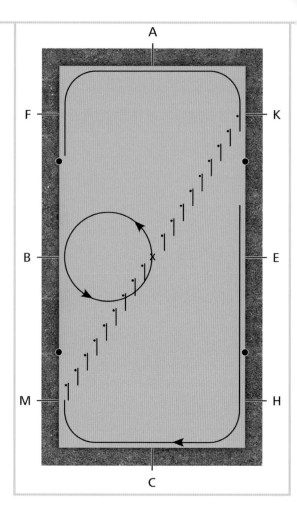

slightly left (away from the direction of travel) with your left rein. Use your right rein to guide the horse onto the diagonal and also to limit the amount of left flexion. Your right leg should assume the "guarding" position to make sure your horse's haunches don't lead the rest of his body as you travel across the arena. The horse should remain nearly parallel to the long side, with his shoulders moving only minimally ahead of the hindquarters.

2 Leg-yield to X, and prepare to ride a volte to the left. Bring your left leg to the forward-driving position at the girth and weight both seat bones evenly until the horse moves straight ahead rather

than sideways. Since you are immediately turning onto a volte, you must once again increase the weight on your left seat bone, but in this case the left seat bone should push *forward*. In the leg-yield, the left seat bone pushes the horse *forward-and-sideways* to the right.

3 On the volte, the outside (right) "guarding" leg and the outside rein prevent the horse from drifting outward. The inside (left) leg keeps the horse moving actively forward, and the inside rein helps direct the horse on the line of travel while establishing inside flexion.

4 As soon as you complete the volte on your return to X, move your left leg behind the girth and weight your left seat bone so it directs the horse forward-and-sideways to the right, beginning the leg-yield again.

5 Increase outside (right) rein until the horse is no longer bent laterally through his body but is only flexed to the left at the poll. The inside (left) rein is responsible for creating the flexion.

6 Your right leg prevents the horse's haunches from swinging "outside" to the right, and together with the left leg, it helps send the horse forward-and-sideways.

7 Prepare to end the leg-yield when you reach the track at the end of the diagonal (at M or K). Straighten your horse and send him forward with equal driving aids on both sides.

8 Practice the exercise in both directions!

Leg-Yield-Straight-Leg-Yield Across the Diagonal

Where You Go

Ride in walk on the track on the right rein. As you ride out of the second corner on the short side and onto the long side (at M or K), ask your horse to leg-yield away from the track (toward the centerline) off your left leg. Leg-yield for four steps. Then, straighten your horse and ride straight ahead on a line parallel to the track for four steps. Repeat the leg-yield off the left leg for four more steps, then a straight line for four steps, and so on. When you get close to the end of the arena, end the exercise by riding straight ahead toward the track on the short side and tracking left upon reaching it. Note: This exercise is designed to be ridden in a 20- by 60-meter arena, as pictured in the diagram, or in an even larger riding space, rather than the small, 20- by 40-meter arena (see p. 19). In the small arena there is too little room to leg-yield as required in this exercise.

Why You Do It

This exercise tests whether horse and rider can change direction of travel (*forward* to *forward-and-sideways*) fluidly after a predetermined number of strides. Alternating so frequently between moving forward and forward-and-sideways requires the horse to respond promptly to the rider's aids. The rider's ability to coordinate when to *give* and *release* the aids will improve, and the horse's flexibility and balance improves as he alternates between crossing his legs

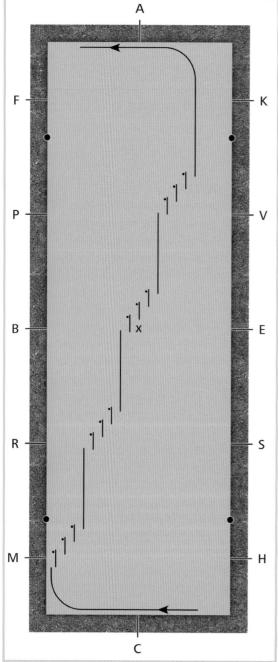

A

F   K

P   V

B   x   E

R   S

M   H

C

Here's How

1 Ride through the short side of the arena in walk, tracking right.

2 After you leave the second corner (at M or K) shift your weight more onto your left seat bone. Both legs should be positioned slightly behind the girth. Use the left leg to drive your horse sideways and both legs to keep the horse moving forward. The right leg prevents the haunches from drifting "out" or ahead of the forehand. The left rein should be used at the start of the leg-yield to establish the inside (left) flexion. The right rein limits the flexion and prevents the horse from "falling through" the right shoulder.

3 Once your horse begins to leg-yield, count out four steps.

4 After the fourth step of leg-yield, ride your horse straight ahead, parallel to the track, as if aiming for a distant, imaginary point on the short side of the arena: Weight both your seat bones evenly. Steadily increase the use of your right seat bone until both seat bones are weighted evenly and the horse moves straight ahead. Position both legs at the girth and send the horse forward, keeping him straight between both reins.

5 Ride a total of four steps straight toward your imaginary point.

6 Begin to leg-yield again—another four steps. Now that your horse no longer has the "support" of the fence or wall along the track it is more difficult to keep him parallel to the long side as you move forward-and-sideways. Horses often trail with their haunches (and neglect to cross their legs sufficiently) or lead with the haunches when leg-yielding off the rail like this. The rider must adjust the leg aids appropriately to remedy such issues.

and traveling straight ahead. This exercise is well suited to solving a lateral tendency in the walk. Moving forward-and-sideways forces the horse to have a pure four-beat walk rhythm, which the rider can then try to maintain as they travel straight ahead for a few steps.

7 Continue alternating leg-yield and straight repetitions until you reach the short side of the arena. Track left and try the exercise again, now this direction.

8 This exercise can also be ridden in a trot—the horse's stride will need to be shortened.

Having Problems?

- *Your horse continues stepping sideways after you ask him to travel straight ahead.* Your horse is "falling through" the outside shoulder. Use your outside aids very clearly, and ride forward with more energy. This problem can also occur if your horse has memorized this exercise and is anticipating the next movement. Be assertive and don't allow your horse to take over!

Leg-Yield Center-line to Track and Canter

Where You Go

Ride in walk, tracking right, onto the short side, and turn up the centerline. Leg-yield your horse off the right leg toward the track. (Note: The leg-yield should begin in the first third of the centerline.) Upon reaching the track, ride a transition to right lead canter.

Why You Do It

As in Exercise 11 (see p. 48), this exercise helps prepare the horse for the transition from walk to canter. The horse is suppled on the inside (right) rein, the inside flexion improves, and the horse is "sent into" the outside (left) rein making it possible for the rider to soften the inside rein in the moment of the canter transition. This allows the horse's inside hind leg to reach forward, well under the horse's body, with good activity in the transition. (Just to clarify: The outside hind is the first leg to strike off in the canter depart.)

Here's How

1 Ride at the walk, tracking right, and when you come onto the short side of the arena, turn up the centerline at A or C.

2 Ride a few steps straight on the centerline before beginning to leg-yield to the left—off your right leg. If you leg-yield directly out of the turn, the horse may "fall through" his outside (left) shoulder.

3 Increase the weight on your right (inside) seat bone, along with the use of your forward-and-sideways driving right

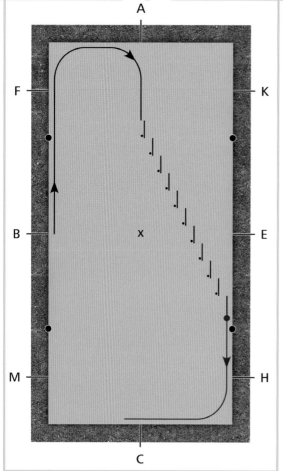

A

F • • • • K

B • x • E

M • • H

C

side flexion. Your right seat bone should remain more heavily weighted than the left, but it now "swings" in a forward direction rather than forward-and-sideways. Even when you are riding in an arena with a wall or fence that prevents the horse from continuing the leg-yield, it is important to actively use the aids to end the leg-yield in order to prepare for the canter transition that comes next in this exercise. These aids should be ideally applied in one step while also giving a half-halt.

6 Become passive for a brief moment with the driving aids, then ask the horse to canter by pushing your right (inside) seat bone forward, sliding your left (outside) leg back, and giving on the right (inside) rein concurrently. It is important that you do not lose focus after completing the leg-yield (Step 5), because then the "positive tension" that the horse has built up as he moved from the centerline to the track will go to waste.

7 Send your horse forward in the canter by driving with your right leg, *not* your left (inside leg, not outside). Overuse of the outside leg in canter sends the horse's haunches to the inside. If there is a mirror in the corner on the short side of the arena, it is easy to check if your horse's haunches have fallen in as you canter down the track toward it.

8 Repeat this exercise a few times in each direction.

leg to send your horse forward and to the left. Give and take on the right rein to flex your horse to the right.

4 When necessary, use your left rein and left "guarding" leg to keep your horse's left shoulder and haunches from falling too much to the left. As a reminder, your horse's body should remain nearly parallel to the track as he moves, with his forehand leading just slightly.

5 When you reach the track on the long side of the arena, end the leg-yield. Use your left (outside) leg to prevent the horse from stepping further sideways. Return your right (inside) leg to the girth and continue to drive the horse into the outside rein, maintaining a minimal in-

My horse is leg-yielding off my right leg from the centerline toward the track. You can see my slightly opening outside (left) rein to initially guide Adele sideways off the centerline and her increasing softenness at the poll as the leg-yield progresses.

Leg-Yield Track to Centerline and Canter

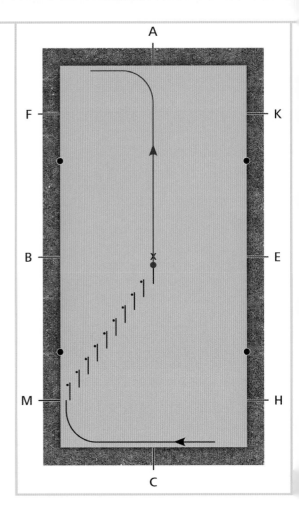

Where You Go

This exercise essentially reverses the movements from the previous exercise (Exercise 22). Ride in the walk onto the short side of the arena, tracking right. After the second corner on the short side, leg-yield your horse from M or K toward the centerline off your left leg. (Note: Your left leg is on the *outside* of the arena, but the *inside* of the horse's flexion.) Upon reaching the centerline, straighten the horse and ride a transition to left-lead canter. When you reach the end of the centerline at A or C, track left on the short side.

Why You Do It

In addition to the benefits gained in Exercise 22 (see p. 71), this exercise requires and tests even more precision from the rider, especially as it relates to the canter transition. Are you able to keep your horse straight in the canter transition without any help from the arena wall or fence? Can you canter down the centerline without "wiggling and wavering"?

Here's How

1 After you walk through a *correct corner* from the short side onto the long side on the right rein, begin the leg-yield off your left leg at M or K.

2 Leg-yield until you reach the centerline around X, using the aids described in Exercise 21 (see p. 69).

3 Once on the centerline, end the leg-yield with a half-halt to balance the horse, straighten him, and send him forward with both seat bones weighted: Return your left leg to the girth while keeping your right leg in the "guarding" position to prevent the horse's haunches from "falling out" to the right. Apply your right rein to straighten him. In this moment, allow the horse to build "positive tension" in order to prepare for the canter depart.

4 After organizing the horse with the half-halt, become passive with your aids for an instant. Then ask for the left-lead canter by pushing your left hip forward while holding the right rein steadily. The less leg aid you use, the better the chance your horse will remain straight during the canter depart on the centerline.

5 Fix your gaze down the centerline on A or C at the opposite end. Use your weight aids to drive the horse forward in a straight line as your legs also lightly enclose him to prevent drifting. Half-halt only as often as is needed to keep the horse steady in the contact. *Do not attempt to keep him straight on the centerline by "steering" him with the reins!*

6 At the end of the centerline track left, and repeat the exercise in both directions.

Having Problems?

● *Your horse responds lackadaisically to your canter aid, perhaps coming above the bit and off the aids in the process.* Practice canter departs from the walk at easier locations in the ring, such as on a circle or on the rail as in Exercise 22, until the transition is more confirmed. It is important to prepare the horse well for canter transitions but not to become so insistent that he becomes tense and unhappy. This can lead to the horse becoming "stuck" in the canter transition as he loses the desire to go sufficiently forward.

● *Your horse becomes crooked in the canter transition or as you travel along the centerline.* Fix your gaze on the letter at the end of the centerline and do not look away! Also make sure to ride sufficiently forward. When you ride unnecessarily slowly it becomes more difficult for your horse to maintain his balance.

Leg-Yield Track to Centerline, Ride a Figure Eight, Leg-Yield Back to Track

Where You Go

This exercise is best suited for a 20- by 60-meter dressage ring. It is possible to ride it in the small 20- by 40-meter arena, but the leg-yield must be done at a very steep angle. Begin by riding in walk, tracking right along the short side by A. After coming through the second corner, at K, begin to leg-yield your horse off your left leg, away from the track and toward the centerline. Ride forward-and-sideways at an angle that ensures your horse reaches the centerline one or two strides before X—not at X or after it. At X, ride a 10-meter volte to the left and then a 10-meter volte to the right (a figure eight). When the figure eight at X is complete, leg-yield back to the track off the right leg. You should reach the track at H.

Why You Do It

This exercise is another variation on the leg-yielding theme. Adding a figure eight between leg-yields in both directions increases the horse's suppleness of body and promotes a relaxed state of mind. This is a good exercise to use in the warm-up, as the figure eight helps achieve initial lateral bend in the horse. This exercise may also help horses that struggle to maintain a clear four-beat rhythm in walk. The frequent changes between the elements of the exercise help improve the horse's flexibility, in-

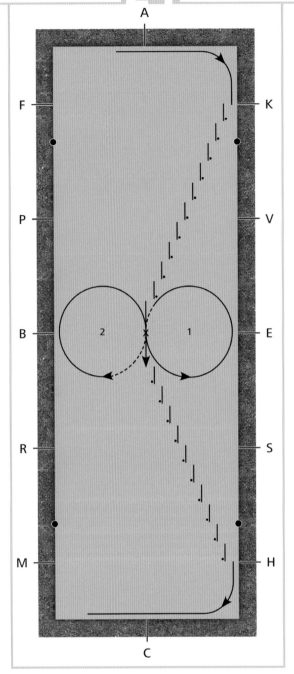

by A, ride at a walk on the right rein through the second corner. Use a half-halt to prepare for the leg-yield.

2 At K, begin to leg-yield the horse off your left leg toward the centerline. Keep an eye on your end point of X, and plan your leg-yield so that you arrive at the centerline one or two strides before it.

3 End your leg-yield by driving the horse's hind legs increasingly forward into your hands. Use both seat bones and both legs. Be prepared to give a strong leg aid with both calves if your horse continues to drift sideways.

4 Once your horse is straight on the centerline (ideally at X), begin your volte to the left. Bring your left (inside) hip forward and your left shoulder back. Keep the horse stepping actively with your left leg positioned at the girth as your left rein establishes the flexion and guides the horse onto the volte. The right (outside) rein and right "guarding" leg prevent the horse's outside shoulder and his hindquarters from drifting out. A volte with a diameter of 10 meters that begins at X touches the track at E and ends again at X. To the observer, it should appear that the first volte is ridden directly out of the leg-yield. This means that the end of the leg-yield and the preparation for the volte (which ends up being the same thing) must occur very efficiently, lasting for only the one or two straight steps before X.

5 As you complete the volte and approach X again, prepare your horse for the upcoming change of direction with a half-halt. Momentarily straighten the horse as you pass "over" X, and then use your right leg, which should now be positioned at the girth, to drive the horse into the left rein so he can be lighter on

crease his focus, and maintain his attention, as well as offering the rider an opportunity to fine-tune her aids.

Here's How

1 Beginning on the short side of the arena

the right rein as you switch direction. Your left leg should slide backward but maintain contact with the horse's side to ensure that the hind legs follow in the same track as the front legs. Once your horse is balanced, begin the volte to the right.

6 Bring your right (now inside) hip forward and your right shoulder back. Obtain the flexion with your right rein while guiding the horse into the turn. The left (now outside) rein allows for the flexion and the turn. Your right leg should continue to drive at the girth and your right rein should be repeatedly softened during the volte so the horse does not lean on it.

7 Once you finish the volte to the right (passing "over" X), increase your left (outside) aids to decrease the horse's lateral bend. Just keep a slight amount of flexion to the right for the upcoming leg-yield. As you leave the volte you must also ask your horse to become more active behind and shorter in his entire outline. Otherwise he will lack the "positive tension" necessary for performing a correct leg-yield, and mistakes—such as "falling through" the outside shoulder—may occur.

8 Begin the leg-yield off the right leg and back toward the track. Keep H in your peripheral vision as the ending point. Upon reaching the track at H, straighten the horse—remember, you need to use your aids to straighten him; don't just rely on the wall or fence to do it.

9 Practice in both directions. This exercise can also be ridden at the trot.

Lengthen Between Leg-Yields

Where You Go

Ride in working trot along the track on the right rein. As you turn onto the long side of the arena at M, ask the horse to leg-yield three to four steps to the right, away from the track. Ride straight ahead, parallel to the track, and lengthen the horse's stride at the trot. Near the circle point before F, return to working trot while leg-yielding the horse to the left, so you are back on the track at F with enough time to ride a *correct corner* onto the short side.

Why You Do It

The leg-yield encourages the horse to step farther underneath his center of gravity and thus improves the "pushing power" of the hindquarters just before you ask the horse to lengthen his stride. This exercise is especially well suited to horses that have not had much previous experience lengthening the stride in trot, as it helps avoid hurried "running": Even though the horse may not be ready for a whole long side of lengthening in trot, the exercise encourages several correct steps. The leg-yield after the lengthening encourages the horse's inside hind leg to remain active and prevents the horse from leaning on your hands and coming onto his forehand as you make the transition back to working trot. This keeps the horse in "self-carriage," eventually enabling his "pushing power" to develop into "carrying capacity." Over time you and your horse will be able to perform an expressive medium trot.

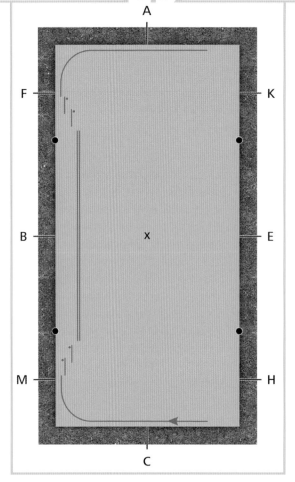

Here's How

1 Ride in working trot, tracking right. Note: If you are schooling an advanced or experienced horse, you can begin in collected trot for added challenge during the trot lengthening.

2 As you turn onto the long side of the arena, ride a half-halt to prepare for the first leg-yield at M. Flex the horse slightly left, and use your left leg behind the girth and increased weight on your left seat bone to ask the horse to travel forward-and-sideways for three or four strides away from the track. Your right rein and right "guarding" leg keep the horse straight with his body aligned nearly parallel to the track. If the hind-quarters swing to the right and begin to lead the leg-yield, the "guarding" aids must come into play more actively.

3 After three or four strides of leg-yield, straighten the horse with a half-halt, returning both legs to the girth and increasing the use of your right seat bone and right rein. This half-halt also increases the horse's "positive tension."

4 Then ask the horse to lengthen his stride in trot. Drive with both legs and both seat bones in rhythm with the trot. Do not sit heavily, "shoving" the horse with your seat. Think of sitting softly and encouraging the horse by "swinging" your hips, as if bringing your lower abdomen forward-and-upward during each stride.

5 Maintain a steady contact with the horse's mouth, elastically following with your arms and hands with each stride. This connection is important to keeping "positive tension" in the horse. While you do not want to "throw the reins away," a slight "giving" of the hand is necessary to accomplish the desired lengthening of the frame. The giving hand should not lose the connection to the horse's mouth, but a too-strong, unyielding contact is unproductive since it prohibits the horse from stretching into the contact, developing impulsion, and "swinging" over his back.

6 With enough room before the end of the long side—when you are even with the circle point on the rail—ask the horse to come back to working (or collected, if appropriate for his level of training) trot. Contain the horse's "pushing power" by giving and taking rein aids and following his movement with your core. Do not expect that your horse will immediately return to the exact pace you desire. Reduce the pace step by step, always "giving" briefly between half-halts.

7 Leg-yield the horse off your right leg back to the track by increasing the weight on your right seat bone and using a forward-and-sideways-driving right leg. The right rein establishes a slight right flexion, while the left rein limits the amount of flexion and guides the horse to the left.

8 Continue to reduce the pace of the trot in the leg-yield. The better the rider can combine these two elements (change of pace and leg yield), the better the horse will keep weight on his hindquarters, stay connected back to front, and remain correct in the contact.

9 When you reach the track around F, straighten your horse with a half-halt and trot through the short side of the arena. Repeat the exercise a few times in each direction. Note that in general, horses tend to move more forward in the lengthening once they are familiar with the exercise.

A dynamic medium trot parallel to the long side; however, my mare has become somewhat too short in the neck. A "give" with the hands will allow her head to come forward and she will "swing" more over the back.

Serpentines

Serpentines are very versatile school figures. They can be used to loosen and supple the horse during warm-up, and they can also be integrated into exercises later in a session to introduce collection. A serpentine can be ridden as a simple single or double loop, or you can make use of the whole arena with various numbers of loops.

As the name implies, the "serpentine" figure has a curved form, which requires a change of bend with each change of direction. Serpentines with *fewer loops* through the arena have a *loosening* and *suppling* effect on the horse, whereas *more loops* produce a *collecting* effect. An even number of loops results in a *change of direction*, while an odd number of loops keeps the horse and rider tracking the same *direction* as before.

The initial change of bend from left to right in a shallow-loop serpentine.

The first loop of a serpentine should begin at the middle of one short side (at A or C), and the last loop should end at A or C on the opposite short side. Each loop should be ridden as a half-volte combined with a straight line, perpendicular to the centerline.

The FN (German Equestrian Federation) stipulates that a shallow-loop serpentine of one loop ridden on the long side of the arena should come 5 meters (about 16.5 feet) off the track at the widest point, while a two-loop serpentine on the long side should come 2.5 meters (approximately 8.25 feet) off the track at the widest part of each loop (see diagram on p. 82 for example). Of course, you can deviate from the "official" size and shape of the serpentines you use to suit specific training purposes, as long as you are at least familiar with their standard form.

We display clearly visible right bend in our serpentine loop.

Now we are changing the bend to the left before reaching the track.

Shallow-Loop Serpentine in Trot, Transition to Walk to Change the Bend

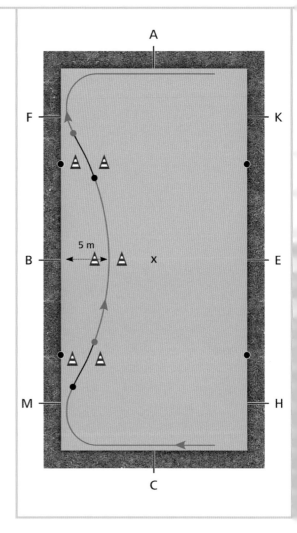

Where You Go

To prepare for this exercise, place six cones along the M-B-F long side in the arena, as shown in the diagram: two cones (with room between for your horse to pass through) approximately even with each circle point (this is where the horse's bend should be changed) and two cones between B and X so that the path of your serpentine is 16.5 feet (5 meters) off the track. The cones will help you ride a symmetrical and correctly shaped loop successfully.

Ride on the track in trot, tracking right. After the second corner of the short side by C, turn off the track at M as if you are about to ride across the diagonal. Your horse should be flexed and bent to the right. Steer toward the first set of cones. Shortly before the cones ride a transition to walk. Walk through the cones, picking up the trot again right after. Use the steps of walk to give you time to change your horse's flexion and bend—from right to left. Trot the loop with the horse bent left, passing through the second set of cones in trot. Directly before the last set of cones, ride another transition to walk. As you walk through the cones change the flexion and bend back to the right and pick up the trot again. End the movement by returning to the track at F. Your horse should sort of "snake" through the cones.

Why You Do It

The cones ensure that you ride each half of the serpentine loop evenly and that you come the proper distance off the track in the middle. The first and third sets of cones help remind the rider to show a clear change of lateral bend. A mistake that is commonly seen in the shallow-loop serpentine is that other than the very middle of the loop, the horse remains completely straight, without any sign of inside flexion and bending. The transition to the walk prior to the cones gives the rider sufficient time to ride a correct change of lateral bend.

Here's How

1 Begin tracking right on the short side of the arena by C. After you ride a *correct corner*, turn off the track at M. Your right (inside) leg should drive at the girth as you bring your right hip forward and your right shoulder back. Obtain right flexion with your right rein. Your left (outside) leg remains behind the girth in the "guarding" position; the left rein softens enough to allow for the turn, but offers enough support that the horse doesn't "fall through" his outside (left) shoulder or remain "stuck" to the track. Turn off the track at M at an angle similar to the angle at which you would turn to ride across the diagonal. The difference is that instead of riding straight, you are riding a curved line.

2 Direct your horse toward the first set of cones, across from the first circle point. Use a half-halt to prepare for a transition to walk. During the transition, maintain flexion and bend to the right, but once walking, change your horse's flexion and bend to the *left* by weighting your left seat bone more heavily than the right; switching your forward-driving right leg to a "guarding" leg position; sliding your left leg forward toward the girth; and establishing left flexion with the left rein. If your horse is inattentive to your bending aids or comes above the bit, allow yourself more time to change the bend by riding straight for several strides before asking for bend in the new direction. Don't forget to keep your horse stepping actively from behind— otherwise, he will lose his balance and lean on your hands, leading to other problems during the change of bend.

3 Once you have passed through the first set of cones and achieved a left lateral bend, ride a transition back to trot. Begin riding the serpentine loop to the left, which will pass through the second set of cones. The horse should be flexed and bent to a degree relative to your curved line of travel. Since the loop in this exercise is fairly shallow, the degree of bend and flexion is fairly little. Make sure that each half of the curve is even: Do not ride the first half as a straight line and then the second as a very curved line. Use the outside (right) aids to keep your horse from drifting off the desired line.

4 Before the last set of cones at the second circle point, ride another transition to walk while maintaining the left flexion and bend. Remember that you are now on your way back to the track, and the angle at which you approach the track should be the same as that which you left the track in the first part of the loop (Step 1). Imagine that you are riding a mirror image of the first half of the exercise. As you pass through the cones, ask your horse for a clear change of bend from left to right. Keep your horse "together": This exercise is a bit of an exception as you do not need to ride a very ground-covering walk.

5 After changing the bend to the right, ride a transition to trot and continue along the curved line of the serpentine until reaching the track. Note that this segment of the serpentine is so short and flat that it is barely recognizable as a curved line. A correctly ridden shallow-loop serpentine should create a harmonious impression as it has a gynmasticizing effect on the horse.

6 When your horse can show fluid changes of bend after riding this exercise several times in both directions, try riding the whole thing in trot.

Shallow-Loop Serpentine in Canter with Simple Changes

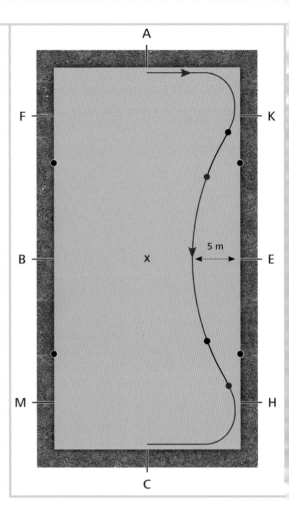

Where You Go

The shape of this exercise is exactly the same as in the previous exercise (Exercise 26): Ride on the track in canter, tracking right and on the right lead, and make a shallow-loop serpentine on the long side of the arena, beginning at K. At the circle point where you should show the first change of bend, ride a simple change of lead—transition down to the walk before picking up the canter again. Ride the center part of the serpentine loop in left-lead canter. Before reaching the track at H, ride another simple change, and pick up the right lead again.

Why You Do It

This exercise offers the chance to school simple changes of lead in an "unusual" location (off the track; not on the diagonal) to add variety to training. By turning off the track, it is easier for the rider to bring the horse down to a walk and then perform a successful upward transition back to canter. As the horse turns back toward the track for the second walk transition at the circle point before H, the approaching arena wall or fence will encourage the horse to naturally "rock" back, shifting his weight onto his hind end. Since this exercise takes place primarily off the track, the rider is required to keep the horse correctly between the aids so the horse doesn't "fall in" or "fall out." Note: This exercise is not well suited to introducing simple changes of lead to the horse for the first time. Before riding this exercise, horse and rider should already be comfortable with simple changes in other parts of the arena.

Here's How

1   After you canter on the right rein along the short side of the arena at A, come out of the second corner onto the long side, and begin riding a shallow-loop serpentine at K. Keep your horse flexed and bent to the right. Push your right seat bone forward, drive with your right leg at the girth while also using your left leg in the "guarding" position behind the girth to prevent the horse's hindquarters from remaining "stuck" on the track and keep the horse moving actively forward.

The right rein obtains the flexion and guides the horse off the track, while the left rein limits the flexion inside (right) in order to prevent the outside (left) shoulder from "bulging out."

2 Once you have left the track, ride a preparatory half-halt and then a transition to walk. Walk for five or six steps on a light contact so the horse maintains a correct rhythm; however, don't allow the horse to completely fall apart in the walk or he will lack the "positive tension" required for the transition back to canter.

3 While in the walk, flex your horse left (now the inside). Drive your horse into the right (now the outside) rein with your left leg. Supple your horse to the left by giving and taking briefly and gently on the left rein.

4 Push your left seat bone forward and slide your right leg back to ride a transition to canter. Soften your left rein to allow for the first stride of canter.

5 Ride the curve of the shallow-loop serpentine in collected, left-lead canter. There will only be room for a few canter strides before it is time for you to ride the next walk transition. Use many half-halts to ask your horse to step well underneath himself with his hind legs, creating an energetic and "uphill" canter, out of which you could ride a transition to walk at any time.

6 As you approach the circle point before H, ask for the transition to walk. Ride three to five steps of walk and then transition to right-lead canter *before* reaching the track at H. Ask for the upward transition as described in Step 4, just reverse the aids. Maintain right flexion and bend as you return to the track and enter the first corner on the short side.

Shallow-Loop Serpentine with a Volte at X

Where You Go
Ride in trot tracking left along the short side of the arena by A. Begin a shallow-loop serpentine at F. Change bend at the circle point following F and ride all the way to the middle of the arena so the center of your serpentine loop touches X. Note that X is farther off the track than you have gone in previous serpentine exercises (about 33 feet or 10 meters). At X ride a 10-meter volte, touching the track at the letter B. After completing the volte, continue on the second half of the serpentine, changing bend from right to left at the circle point before M, and entering the track again at M in time to ride the first corner of the short side.

Why You Do It
Since this serpentine has a more clearly curved form than the serpentines in the previous exercises, it is even better suited to schooling change of lateral bend. Horses that tend to brace against the rider's inside leg in the curve in order to avoid bending can be corrected using this exercise. The volte in the middle of the loop further supports the rider's efforts to achieve correct flexion and bend, and then the newly acquired bend is already in place for the second loop back to the track.

Here's How
1 On the left rein, trot through the short side of the arena past A. The exercise can be ridden in collected trot or working trot.

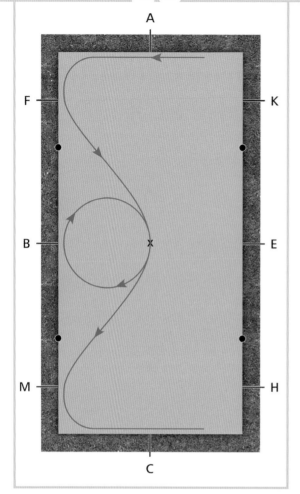

carriage with a steady right lateral bend. Shortly before X, collect the horse and ride 10-meter volte to the right. Since the path of the volte is more curved than the path of the serpentine, you must prepare the horse by increasing his level of collection and uphill balance. Use your driving aids to ask the horse's hind legs to step farther underneath his body and shorten the reins, especially the inside (right) rein, in order to create the inside flexion. The rider's inside leg should be positioned at the girth while the outside (left) leg should be slightly farther back. Both legs drive the horse forward and keep the hind legs following along the same path as the forelegs. Of course, the exact aids vary according to each horse's specific needs and the direction of travel. Many horses require the use of stronger outside aids while traveling in one direction to prevent the hindquarters from *swinging out*, while they tend to *fall in* with the hindquarters in the opposite direction. Over-bending the horse to the inside only allows the horse's outside shoulder to "bulge out" and exacerbates the problem of the haunches coming to the inside.

2 After leaving the second corner of the short side, begin your serpentine at F on the long side. Note your first curve requires a steeper angle than those in Exercises 26 and 27 because you want to touch the centerline at X.

3 When you are even with the first circle point, change your horse's flexion and bend from left to right, and focus on riding all the way to X at the center of the loop. An observer should now be able to recognize a clearer change of bend than in the previous serpentine exercises.

4 As you ride the curve to the right use half-halts while activating the horse's hind legs so the horse remains in self-

5 Use the volte to school the horse's right lateral bend, then continue on to the second half of the serpentine with a degree of bend relative to the curve of the path of travel. The serpentine needs less bend and flexion than the volte, so decrease the horse's lateral bend to the right by taking a firmer hold of the left (outside) rein and diminishing the use of your right (inside) weight aids.

6 When you are even with the next circle point, flex your horse to the left and acquire left lateral bend relative to the degree of curve of your line of travel. Continue toward the letter M on the track.

Adding a volte in the middle of a shallow-loop serpentine offers an opportunity to school increased flexion and lateral bend.

7 As you reach M, straighten your horse and again trot along the track and onto the short side.

8 Repeat the exercise in both directions.

Shallow-Loop Serpentine in Canter, No Lead Changes

Where You Go

Ride in collected canter tracking left around the short side of the arena by A. (Note: It is wise to begin this exercise in the direction in which your horse canters more easily. This explanation assumes the left lead is the easier side for the horse.) On the long side of the arena, begin to ride a very "flat" (limited curve to the loops) shallow-loop serpentine—it should be less than 16.5 feet (5 meters) off the track between B and X. Maintain the left lead through the entire serpentine.

Why You Do It

This exercise helps prepare the horse and rider for counter-canter—where the horse is flexed and bent the opposite of the curve of the line of travel and on the opposite lead of the "true" canter. The bend in the serpentine in this exercise introduces the horse to cantering on the counter lead on a curved line while maintaining his balance. Since the horse only counter-canters briefly before returning to the track in true canter, the possibility of the horse switching leads without being asked is greatly reduced. The degree of difficulty is low in this case, since the loop of the serpentine is quite shallow; however, the difficulty can be increased at any time by increasing the size of the loop and riding farther away from the track. In general, schooling the horse in counter-canter improves straightness and collection.

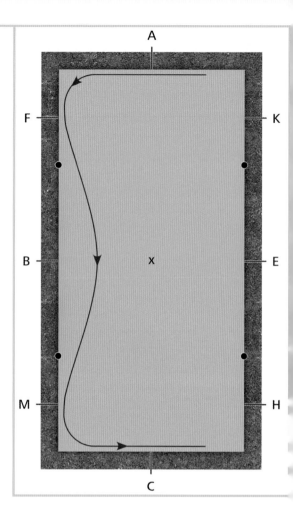

Here's How

1   Track left, and ride in collected canter on the left lead. Use frequent half-halts to make sure the horse remains in self-carriage as you come around the short side by A. You can check to see whether the horse is "carrying himself" by subtly—or occasionally more obviously—giving the reins forward.

2   On the long side at F leave the track at a slight angle and begin the first shallow curve of your serpentine.

3   As you canter on the slight curve between the track and centerline, keep your horse fairly straight in his neck but still flexed to the left. From time to time play on the right rein to keep your horse

supple at the poll, but not so much that you inspire him to switch leads. Sit clearly positioned for the left-lead canter: your left seat bone forward, your left leg driving at the girth, and your right leg back behind the girth.

4 Near the second circle point on the long side, guide your horse back to the track, aiming to be there at M. Continue to sit with your seat and legs very clearly positioned for the left lead canter. Make sure that your horse feels your right leg positioned behind the girth. Take and soften briefly on the left rein to keep slight left flexion. In the moments when you soften the left rein, use the right rein to guide the horse's shoulders outward, making a gentle curve back to the track—you can even use an opening right rein if necessary.

5 Practice the exercise in both directions. You can gradually increase the challenge by making the curved path of the serpentine loop more significant—eventually "touching" X in the middle as in Exercise 28 (see p. 85).

Having Problems?

- *Your horse "falls apart" in the loop of the serpentine, leaning on your hand or breaking into trot.* Your horse is probably lacking forward energy and "throughness" in canter. Before trying this exercise again, work to improve the horse's collected canter by riding many walk-canter-walk transitions. Then canter the loop of the serpentine, but add in a transition to walk halfway through (between B and X, if riding according to the scenario described in Steps 1 through 4). As soon as the horse walks, immediately transition back to canter. This will remind the horse to listen to your balancing half-halts during the serpentine. Then repeat the exercise without the walk-canter-walk transition. Use many half-halts to ensure that the horse remains in self-carriage. Give the horse a sufficient walk break after several attempts.

- *Your horse constantly swaps leads.* Do not punish him! If you teach him that flying changes (changing lead without transitioning downward to walk or trot) are a punishable offense, you will have difficulty later on when you want to train the flying changes. This issue, like the problem described prior, requires further development of the collected canter. Ride in true canter on a 20-meter circle. Play with the flexion so that you flex your horse slightly to the outside (of the circle) for a few canter strides while continuing to ride along the path of the circle. This will help improve your horse's balance. Then, try Exercise 29 "one step at a time," riding a transition down to the walk as soon as you feel your horse is losing his balance or is about to switch leads. Try to avoid allowing the horse to make mistakes by riding only as many steps of the serpentine in canter as your horse can do correctly, then transitioning to walk. Gradually increase the number of steps before you transition to walk. Praise your horse generously when he tries!

Counter-Canter Benefits
Riding changes of pace within the counter-canter helps improve overall expression, and riding very exactly through corners and on other school figures at the counter-canter increases the degree of collection your horse can maintain.

Three-Loop Serpentine with Walk Transitions

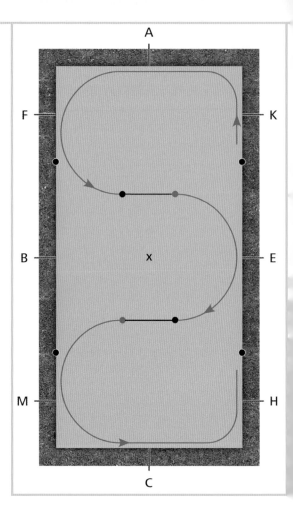

Where You Go

Ride in trot tracking left. Ride a three-loop serpentine from one end of the ring to the other, with a transition to walk and exactly five steps of walk each time you cross the centerline. The third step of each walk segment should occur exactly on the centerline. After the required steps of walk, return to trot and continue on the serpentine.

Why You Do It

Serpentines offer the rider a chance to make good use of the arena while dividing it up into equal sections that are to be ridden accurately. In this exercise, horse and rider have the opportunity to practice making downward transitions to walk at an exact point, precisely riding a predetermined number of steps at the walk, and then accomplishing prompt transitions to trot. This exercise helps prepare the horse and rider for riding a three-loop serpentine at the canter with simple changes over the centerline. And, it also helps improve overall "throughness."

Here's How

1 Before beginning your serpentine at one short side of the arena, plan the size of each loop so that all three loops will be equal. Imagine that each loop consists of a half-circle touching the track, and each loop is connected to the next by a straight line intersecting the centerline at a 90-degree angle. When riding a three-loop serpentine in a 20- by 40-meter arena, each loop will have a width

of approximately 13 meters (42.5 feet). Each circle point on the long side of the arena (if you remember, these are the points where the horse "touches" the track on the long side when ridden on a 20-meter circle on the short side) is 10 meters (33 feet) from the nearest short side and can be used for orientation: You must ride the line connecting the first and second loops in your serpentine 3 meters (10 feet) past the location of the circle point. The second loop is centered on the middle of the long side at E or B. The horse should touch the track briefly at this letter. The same theory applies to the third loop as to the first loop.

Isidor has just left the track in a serpentine loop to the left in working trot.

2 After planning the geometry of your serpentine, ride at the trot along the track on the left rein. Begin to ride the first loop of the serpentine as you reach the midpoint of the short side at A. Increase the weight on your left seat bone, drive with your left leg at the girth, and keep your right leg in the "guarding" position to prevent the hindquarters from drifting out (right). Use additional left rein to obtain inside flexion. Do not ride deeply into the second corner of the short side as you might usually because you are beginning the first loop of your serpentine.

3 To create a correctly rounded first loop your horse should only momentarily touch the track between F and the first circle point.

4 As you complete the left half-turn and head toward the centerline, moving from the first loop into the second, keep your horse straight between both reins and both of your legs. Ride a transition to walk. Use half-halts not only to straighten the horse but also to prepare

him for the downward transition: Both seat bones and both legs positioned at the girth send the horse forward into a briefly holding hand. As soon as the horse begins to walk, soften with both hands so the transition is fluid. Count the steps of walk.

5 Time your aids for the trot so that the horse only walks five steps. *Do not* wait until after the fifth step to give the aids for the upward transition! Use an impulse-like leg aid to ask for the trot, which should be preceded by reestablishing the connection that was softened for the walk in Step 4.

6 As soon as the horse trots, begin the next loop of the serpentine to the right. Bring your right seat bone forward, use your right leg at the girth to keep the horse moving fluidly forward, the right rein obtains the inside flexion, which is limited as necessary by the left rein. The rider's left leg moves into position behind the girth to prevent the horse's haunches from swinging out (to the left). "Touch" the track at E and complete the half-turn of the loop.

7 As you approach the centerline again on the straightaway portion of the second loop of the serpentine, straighten your horse and prepare for your transition to walk. Proceed as described in Step 4.

8 The third loop touches the long side between the second circle point and M— your horse now flexed and bent to the left. This loop of the serpentine ends at the middle of the short side (C), so remember, the first corner of the short side should not be ridden deeply, but as part of a half-circle.

9 Once you and your horse feel comfortable with the exercise in trot, ride it in a canter!

Three-Loop Serpentine with Halts Over the Centerline

Where You Go

Ride in trot, tracking left. Plan and ride a serpentine of three loops from one short end of the arena to the other. Each time you cross the centerline, ride a halt transition, then pick up the trot out of the halt and continue along the serpentine pattern.

Why You Do It

As in Exercise 30 (see p. 90), this exercise requires accurately planned and timed transitions, as well as correct use of and equal division of the space in the arena. It also schools the halt transition without the help of an arena wall, and teaches rider and horse to accomplish prompt transitions to trot from the halt. Riding this exercise improves lateral bend, and it helps the horse step farther underneath himself, balancing more of his weight over his hindquarters before the change of direction. The result is an increase in the horse's ability to collect and improved the "throughness."

Here's How

1 For the most part this exercise is ridden as described in Exercise 30 (see p. 90).

2 Each halt should occur exactly as the horse hits the centerline, and the horse should be adequately prepared with half-halts. Shorten the trot stride as soon as you ride the curved line away from the track. Use seat and leg aids to drive the horse into the repeatedly taking and softening hand. When the half-

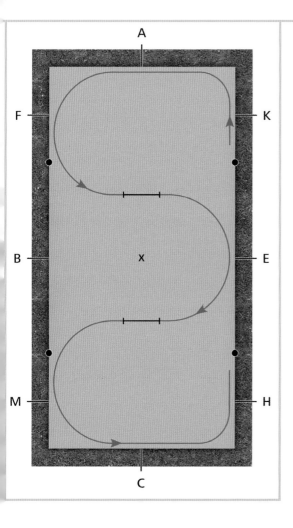

ward movement and sit slightly forward to stay with the horse's motion. Avoid falling behind the horse's motion as he moves off into trot!

6 Continue along the path of the serpentine as described in the previous exercise.

Having Problems?

- *Your horse "dances around" during the halt or repeatedly steps sideways.* Perhaps you have ridden the transition with too much hand or ridden it too abruptly. Try again, this time riding the transitions quite gradually. When your horse stands still, reward him. Gradually ask for clearer transitions again. As soon as the horse halts remember to become light with your hands.

halts have had the desired effect, and you notice that your horse has shortened his trot stride sufficiently, ride the transition to halt. Leave both legs on the horse's sides so he doesn't step backward or sideways. As soon as the horse halts, lighten your hands so as not to cause an undesired step backward.

3 Remain calmly halted for a moment.

4 Regain the horse's attention to prepare for the transition to trot by pushing both hips forward toward a briefly holding hand.

5 Use both legs at the same time to achieve a straight transition into the trot. Soften with both hands to allow for the for-

Three-Loop Serpentine with Cavalletti

Where You Go
To prepare for this exercise, place three ca-valletti along the straight line connecting each loop in a three-loop serpentine (see diagram). Set the cavalletti at a distance appropriate for your horse's trot stride (approximately 3.5 to 4.25 feet or 1.1 to 1.3 meters). Ride in trot tracking right, beginning your serpentine in the middle of the short side at C. Trot over the cavalletti each time you cross the centerline.

Why You Do It
This exercise adds variety to your standard dressage work. You are required to be flexible in your riding position, alternating between the dressage seat the majority of the time and the forward seat as you go over the cavalletti. The horse is required to perform fluid transitions between the straight and curved lines of the serpentine, and the rider needs to be able to straighten the horse efficiently after each curved line as a prerequisite for successfully navigating the cavalletti. This exercise offers an opportunity to build up the horse's muscles along his back and in his hindquarters by allowing him to stretch forward over the cavalletti, then resume a more upright frame in the serpentine loops.

Note: The rider's stirrups should be shortened one or two holes for this exercise.

Here's How
1 Ride in trot, tracking right around the ring.
2 Begin the first loop of the serpentine

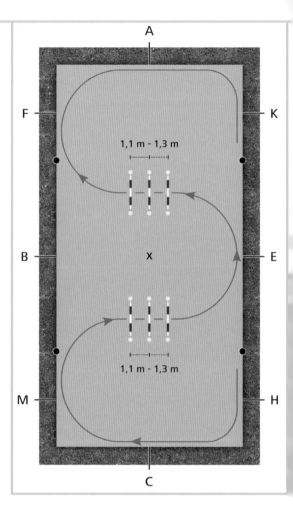

when you reach the middle of the short side at C. Bring your right hip forward and use both legs to keep the horse actively trotting. Your right leg should be positioned at the girth and your left leg behind the girth to prevent the haunches from swinging out (left). The right rein is responsible for the right flexion, and the left rein allows for it.

3 Make your first half-circle turn between M and the first circle point on the long side. As you ride out of the serpentine loop onto the straightaway, headed toward the centerline, immediately straighten your horse: Increase the contact with the left rein, weight both seat bones evenly, and drive the horse for-

ward with both legs positioned at the girth. Fix your gaze on the middle of the first cavalletti.

4 Just before reaching the cavalletti, make sure you have your horse's attention with a half-halt. Maintain the connection that you achieved in the first steps of the exercise.

5 Signal to your horse that he should stretch forward. Sit slightly forward, distributing your weight predominantly into your heels and onto your calves and knees (forward seat). "Give" your hands forward in the direction of the horse's mouth.

6 As you trot over the cavalletti, absorb the horse's movement in your heels. Make sure to give with your hands, and do not let yourself fall behind the motion. (Note, however, that the reins should not be totally slack!) The rider's calves should maintain contact with the horse's sides to keep him between the aids and give him a sense of security. This prevents the horse from hesitating in the last moment or diverting from the desired path ("wiggling" or running out). That said, just because there is a pole in front of you does not mean that you should suddenly create more pressure with your legs! This only causes the horse to rush at the poles, making the distances incorrect, detracting from the rhythm of the movement, and limiting the overall benefits of the exercise.

7 After riding over the cavalletti at the centerline, sit in the saddle again (dressage seat), and immediately drive your horse into a briefly holding hand to bring him back into a working frame. Then begin your serpentine loop to the left.

8 Complete the final loops as described in Exercise 31 (see p. 92), but with the addition of the cavalletti.

Having Problems?

- *The exercise seems too difficult.* Ride it in walk at first. Adjust the distances between cavalletti to fit the walk (2.5 to 3.5 feet or 0.8 to 1.1 meters), and if the cavalletti are adjustable, move them to the lowest option. You can also begin with a single cavalletto on the centerline instead of three, and only increase the number gradually as you and the horse get the hang of the exercise.

- *Your horse runs out to the outside of the cavalletti* (out to the left for example after the loop to the right). Increase the use of your outside rein and leg, and ride the serpentine loop smaller than normal. Shorten your horse's stride so you have more control.

"Ground Poles" or "Cavalletti"?

Whether you use actual cavalletti or simply ground poles really depends only on the availability of each and how practical it is for you to lay them out and put them away when setting up and cleaning up the exercise. Cavalletti offer the advantage that when a horse hits one with a leg it is much less likely to move out of place than a pole, which easily rolls. Cavalletti also tend to command more respect from horses, and this effect can be furthered by varying the cavalletti heights in a single line. Cavalletti also minimize the risk that the horse will step directly onto a pole and injure himself when the pole rolls away. If you do not have cavalletti available, flat-sided poles or planks can be safer choices than your standard round poles.

"Old-Fashioned" Serpentine

Where You Go

Ride in trot around the arena, tracking left. Beginning on the short side at C, ride a five-loop serpentine from one end of the ring to the other. Rather than intersecting the centerline at a right angle as you did in Exercises 30, 31, and 32 (pp. 90, 92, and 94), ride from one loop directly into the "curve" of the next loop without riding a straight line between them. The path of travel forms the characteristic snake-like shape as shown in the diagram.

Why You Do It

This variation of the serpentine tests whether your horse can change direction and lateral bend willingly while remaining on the aids without taking a few straight strides in between to prepare. To perform this exercise well, the horse must be connected from back to front and sufficiently gymnasticized so that he can smoothly change the bend in his body without lengthy preparation. The horse should also be at a stage where he is at least showing early levels of collection.

Here's How

1   Ride along the track on the left rein at the trot. Begin the first serpentine loop on the short side at C. As you come around the second corner, increase the weight on your left seat bone, drive with your left leg at the girth while your right leg "guards" behind the girth to prevent the haunches "falling out." The left rein obtains the flexion and guides the horse around the curve while the right rein softens enough to allow for this.

2   Ride the curved line of the first serpen-

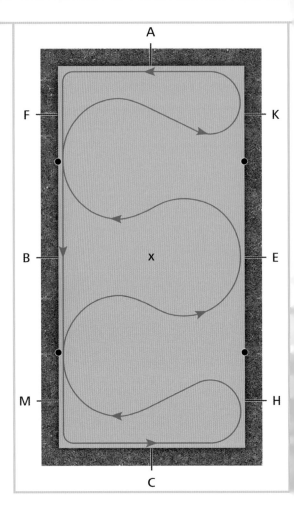

tine loop somewhat farther than normal (more of a three-quarter-circle than a half-circle), and ride out of the loop at an angle toward the centerline. The shape of the loop is similar to that of a tear drop. Maintain a slight left flexion as you approach the centerline.

3   Change your horse's flexion and lateral bend as you cross the centerline. Use a half-halt to ask your horse to step farther under his center of gravity with his hind legs and also to momentarily straighten him. This half-halt should take place during one trot stride. All of the aids should be applied equally on both sides for this half-halt.

4   The release of the half-halt occurs at

the same time as the beginning of the second serpentine loop, now curving to the right. Bring your right hip forward, drive with your right leg at the girth, and move your left leg backward to the "guarding" position to prevent the horse's haunches from "falling out." The left rein controls the horse's left shoulder and allows for the right flexion, which is obtained with the right rein.

5   Ride the subsequent loops in the same manner as described in Steps 1 through 4.

Old vs. New

Many people may wonder why the current form of the figure (such as described in Exercises 30, 31, and 32—pp. 90, 92, and 94) is called a "serpentine" when the "old-fashioned" variation bears much more resemblance to the path made by a slithering reptile! The current version of the serpentine is easier to ride correctly than the earlier version. Dressage schooling figures are also, in principle, movements in dressage tests. And dressage tests are designed to determine whether the horse is on the correct path in his development in accordance with the Classical Training Scale (see p. 4). It was difficult to accurately judge the "old-fashioned" serpentine: From the short side where the judge at C views the horse's profile, it might not be clear whether the horse was tracking straight with his hind feet following in the tracks of his front feet, or whether his hindquarters were swinging to the side during the change of bend and direction. At the canter, it was difficult to judge whether the simple or flying changes at the centerline were straight.

Three-Loop Serpentine with Voltes

Where You Go

Ride on the track in trot, tracking left. Begin a three-loop serpentine at A that goes from one short side of the arena to the other. Each time you and your horse briefly "touch" the track on the long side during a serpentine loop, add in a volte. When the volte is completed, continue the serpentine, adding in another volte in the next loop, and so on.

Why You Do It

This exercise improves the horse's lateral bend and his carrying capacity, as well as serving to correct a common problem: Many horses perform the first loop of the serpentine with correct flexion and bend but proceed to "come against" the rider's inside leg and rein in the next loop (avoiding lateral bend). This loss of control often increases from loop to loop until the horse is no longer on the aids. It is helpful to add in a volte to reestablish control in the location at which the horse tends to lose the bend and flexion: directly in the center of each loop.

Here's How

1   Start at the trot on the short side of the arena at A. Do not ride deeply into the second corner of the short side because this is the beginning of the first loop of your serpentine. You should aim to "touch" the track between F and the circle point on the long side.

2   At this moment, give the aids for a volte to the left. Use a half-halt to prepare the

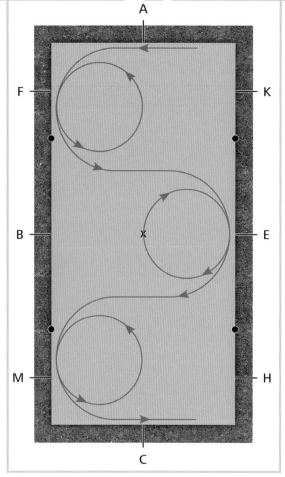

A

F

K

B   x   E

M   H

C

3   Once you have completed the volte pro-
    ceed with the next loop of the serpen-
    tine. The use of your left (inside) rein
    and seat bone as bending aids should
    be slightly diminished in order to remain
    relative to the size of the curved path
    you are traveling.

4   As you ride out of the loop toward the
    centerline, use equal weight, leg, and
    rein aids on both sides to straighten the
    horse.

5   Continue along the serpentine figure,
    adding a volte to the second and third
    loops as well.

Other Ideas for This Exercise
This exercise can be further
modified by adding transitions to
walk or canter at key points in the
figure. For example, ride a downward transition to walk before the
volte, ride the volte in walk, and
then proceed in trot. Or, pick up the
canter as the horse begins the first
loop of the serpentine, canter the
volte, and ride a downward transition to trot at the end of the volte.
Then trot toward the next loop of
the serpentine, where you can pick
up the canter again.

horse for the new task and ride a volte
with a diameter of 10 meters or less. Increase the weight on your left (inside)
seat bone and keep the horse between
the left leg at the girth and the right
(outside) "guarding" leg. The left rein
should obtain the necessary left flexion
and guide the horse along the curved
path of the volte. As soon as your horse
begins to turn onto the volte, "give"
with the left rein so you do not block
the horse's inside hind leg from stepping
forward well under his body. Your outside rein contact should remain steady
to keep the horse's outside shoulder in
line while allowing for the lateral bend
necessary on the volte.

Three-Loop Serpentine in Canter, No Lead Changes

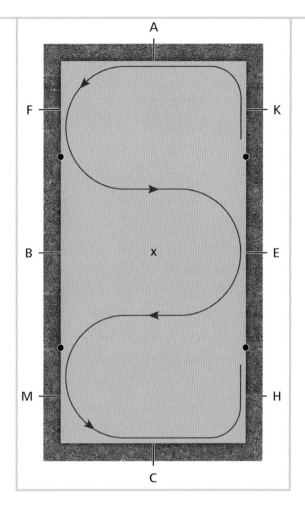

Where You Go

As a prerequisite for this exercise, the horse should be familiar with counter-canter and should be able to collect sufficiently in the canter. Ride in collected canter on the left lead (true canter) along the track. After the short side by A, begin a three-loop serpentine from one end of the arena to the other. Remain on the left lead the entire time—do not allow your horse to switch via simple or flying changes of lead.

Why You Do It

This exercise trains the counter-canter on a bending line. As discussed in Exercise 29 (see p. 88), it is more difficult for your horse to counter-canter on a curved line than on a straight line. The diameter of the half-circle loops on the serpentine is less than that of a 20-meter circle, which adds to the difficulty. On the other hand, the difficulty is decreased by the fact that the horse only counter-canters for a short distance and then seamlessly flows to a true-canter line again.

Here's How

1 Track left in a collected, true canter, and begin the first loop of the serpentine after you pass A on the short side.
2 Use frequent half-halts to ensure that your horse stays light in the contact and maintains activity and impulsion in the collected canter.
3 After the first loop, and as you ride the straight line and approach the second (middle) loop, straighten your horse so that he has only the slightest bit of left flexion. Encourage the horse to take short but energetic canter strides.

4 As you begin the middle loop in counter-canter, make sure to sit clearly positioned for the left lead: Keep your left leg forward at the girth and your right leg back. Your right leg will be more dominant during this loop. Use both reins to guide the horse in and out of the loop. This requires clever, tactful use of the rein aids since the left rein is responsible for the slight left flexion and the right rein steers the horse around the turn. The right rein comes more into play in

Adele and I begin the first loop of a three-loop serpentine, tracking right, in true canter.

the moments when the left rein is giving, and vice versa. However, the horse's flexion should not change when one rein is softened or he will become unbalanced. To encourage the horse to maintain self-carriage, more frequent use of the leg and seat aids are necessary.

5   As you approach the centerline to finish the middle loop, your right leg again assumes the "guarding" function. The left leg should drive the horse increasingly into the right (outside) rein to stabilize the connection so that your left (inside) rein can be light.

6   Complete the third loop and then repeat the exercise in the other direction.

Having Problems?

- *As you ride the turns your horse's canter becomes flat and his head bobs up and down.* Establish a more energetic canter! In this case you may be attempting to collect the canter by using too much hand, the horse hasn't shifted his weight to his hindquarters, and the result is a labored appearance. Unwanted head bobbing also sometimes occurs with young horses. Return to a longer, straighter line and ride energetically forward to reestablish the rhythm.

- *Your horse swaps leads in the second loop.* Use momentarily stronger aids to support your horse. Encourage him to transfer more of his weight to his hindquarters by driving him into a momentarily holding hand and then immediately giving. Maintain a slight left flexion. Alter the geometry of the serpentine so that the first and third loops are small and the middle loop is bigger, which makes it easier for the horse to stay in counter-canter.

Voltes

As with circles and serpentines, voltes are important curved, arena figures. In comparison to a circle, a volte requires an increased degree of lateral bend in the horse due to the volte's smaller diameter—voltes are 6, 8, or 10 meters in diameter. A 10-meter volte can be ridden in a working gait and is therefore part of dressage tests at First and Second Levels. At higher levels, voltes of 8 and 6 meters may appear. Voltes can be ridden in any part of the arena and are therefore very useful and easy to implement in creative ways during dressage schooling.

Ground Poles for Correct Voltes

Where You Go

To prepare for this exercise set a ground pole at a particular volte-diameter's distance from the track—6, 8, or 10 meters (see p. 20 for guidance in measuring meter distances). Trot around the ring at a pace appropriate for the size volte you intend to ride, and ride the volte in the space allowed between the ground pole and the arena wall or fence.

Why You Do It

The ground pole provides a visual reference for the rider so you learn the way each size of volte "feels." The ground pole also serves to form a physical barrier for the horse so that he is discouraged from "falling out" onto a larger volte than is desired by the rider.

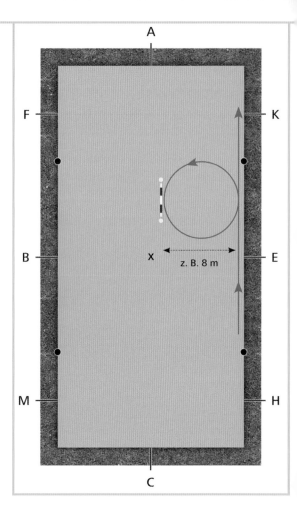

Here's How

1 Trot on the left rein around the arena, toward the point where you have placed the ground pole and would like to begin the volte. Use a half-halt to get your horse's attention.

2 Start your turn left off the track just before the point where you are directly across from the middle of the ground pole. Fix your gaze on the ground pole. Bring your inside (left) hip forward and use your inside leg at the girth to drive your horse into the outside (right) rein. The outside rein should be steady but long enough to allow for the appropriate degree of lateral bend on the path of the volte. The inside rein should be used at the start of the volte to obtain the bend and guide the horse off the track. After that, it should be continuously softened during the completion of the figure so the horse's inside hind leg can step as far as possible under his body and so the horse does not lean on the inside rein and become too deep in the contact. Your outside leg should be in the "guarding" position, behind the girth, to prevent the horse's hindquarters from swinging out. Your outside leg must also help your inside leg maintain the horse's forward momentum and bend.

3 Ride right up to the edge of the ground pole in order to ride the full diameter of the volte.

4 Upon reaching the track again, straighten the horse, and continue on around the arena.

Figure Eight at One End

Where You Go

This exercise works well when ridden in walk or trot. Begin in walk if you are just becoming familiar with the aids and the horse is just learning the desired path of travel. Walk through the short side of the arena by C, tracking right. Ride a 10-meter volte on the right rein at M, in the second corner of the short side. Ride this volte *one-and-a-half times around*. When you reach the centerline again, change your horse's bend from right to left and ride a second 10-meter volte in the opposite corner of the short side. Ride this volte *once around* and when you again reach the centerline, change back to the volte to the right. Repeat several times, and end the exercise by riding straight ahead down the long side the next time you reach the track.

Why You Do It

Frequent changes of direction provide the rider a chance to practice the aids, including redistribution of weight and repositioning of the legs as necessary. The changes of direction also benefit the horse. He will begin to show a clear change of lateral bend while moving smoothly from one volte to the other. The exercise increases the horse's suppleness and "throughness."

Here's How

1 Ride in walk through the short side by C, tracking right. Before reaching M on the long side begin a volte to the right. The volte should reach the centerline to achieve a 10-meter diameter. Another reference point for the correctly sized volte is to imagine a line connecting the

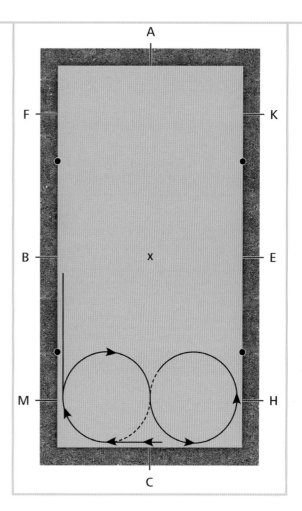

circle points on the far side of M and H—the 10-meter volte should reach as far into the arena as this line "connecting" one long side to the other. This line, the centerline and the segments of the short and long sides form a 10-meter square that encloses your 10-meter volte. Note: It is a common mistake to ride too far out on the open sides of the volte. Make sure this does not happen to you!

2 To start the volte to the right, push your inside (right) hip forward, and drive with your inside leg at the girth and your outside (left) leg behind the girth. The outside leg becomes especially important on the open sides of the arena where there isn't a wall or fence to help

keep the horse from "falling out" on the volte. The inside rein should be somewhat shortened to maintain the inside flexion while the outside rein keeps a steady connection and the horse's outside shoulder in line (another important factor when riding on the open side of the volte where there isn't a wall or fence to support the horse).

3 After you ride one-and-a-half times around the volte to the right, change the horse's bend as you reach the centerline to start the volte to the left. Momentarily straighten the horse exactly at the moment in which you are facing C. In the horse's next step, shift your weight to the left and adjust your legs and reins appropriately. The left rein (now your inside) should be slightly shortened and the right rein (now the outside) allowed to slip through your fingers to a slightly longer length. With practice and improved suppleness, the number of steps in which the horse is ridden straight ahead can be decreased until it is no longer perceivable to an on-looker.

4 Ride a full volte to the left once around and when you come back to the centerline, change directions back to the right volte.

5 Ride several figure eights (combinations of one volte to the left and one to the right), and end the exercise at the same place at which you began—at M. Straighten the horse and use both equally weighted seat bones and both legs positioned at the girth to send the horse forward down the long side.

6 Once you and the horse are comfortable with the exercise in walk, ride it in trot.

Having Problems?

- *Your voltes are shaped like eggs instead of circles.* Keep the reference points in the arena and the "invisible square" described in Step 1 in mind, and work to keep the curved line of travel within those parameters. Horses tend to drift outward in this exercise, especially at the circle points on the long sides. Use your outside rein and outside leg to ride the open side of the circle what seems to be slightly smaller than necessary—then it will usually end up being the correct size! You can also lay out ground poles to create a visible line connecting the circle point on the far side of M to the circle point on the far side of H. This provides a physical barrier to help "contain" the horse on the open side of the volte (see Exercise 36, p. 102).

- *Your horse does not accept the switch from one set of bending aids to the next and "falls" around the turn, counter-flexed.* Clearly take back the pace as you approach the change of direction on the centerline. The shortened stride will make it easier for the horse to maintain his balance. Ride multiple voltes in the same direction if needed in order to obtain correct flexion and bend, before then going ahead and trying the change of direction again. The horse should not be allowed to think that it doesn't need to listen to the bending aids because it is about to change direction anyway. Correct this if it occurs!

Half-Volte Right, Straight, Half-Volte Left

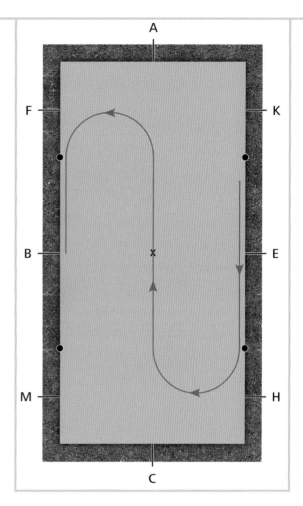

Where You Go

Trot around the arena, tracking right. Ride a 10-meter half-volte beginning at any point of your choice—the circle point before H on the long side is the example depicted in the diagram. You will end up on the centerline after the half-volte. Ride straight ahead on the centerline toward A. Then at a second point of your choice, ride another half-volte, this time to the left, to take you back to the track.

Why You Do It

This exercise offers the horse and rider the opportunity to practice correctly sized voltes, as well as schooling smooth transitions between straight and curved lines. The exercise improves the horse's general "throughness."

Here's How

1 Trot on the track along the long side on the right rein toward the point where you wish to begin the first half-volte—for example, the circle point before H on the long side. Gain your horse's attention and slightly shorten his stride with a preparatory half-halt.

2 Begin the volte by shifting your right (inside) seat bone forward and shortening your right rein to obtain the appropriate inside flexion and to guide the horse off the track. The right leg at the girth and the left (outside) leg in the "guarding" position work together to keep a regular rhythm as the volte begins.

3 Fix your gaze on the centerline by finding the visual reference point of A at the far end of the arena. As soon as the path of the volte meets the centerline straighten your horse. Use half-halts to tell him to step well underneath his body with his hind legs so a very light contact is possible.

4 Begin your turn onto the second half-volte, now to the left, at a previously determined point—for example, when you are across from the circle point before F. Shift your weight to the left (now your inside), adjust the positioning of your legs appropriately, and shorten your left rein. Look at the point at which you will reach the track. Use your right (now your outside) aids to ensure your horse does not "fall" to the outside and so arrive at

the track too early.

5 Once you arrive on the track use a half-halt to straighten the horse and ride actively forward.

6 Repeat the exercise, this time starting from the left rein. This exercise can also be ridden in canter, when you and your horse are ready. Change leads on the centerline, using either a simple or flying change.

New Challenge, Simple Change

Once you have a solid command of this exercise in trot, try it in canter, as well. Use a simple change on the centerline to change leads. Ride around the half-volte as described in Step 2, and head straight onto the centerline. Keep your horse straight between your leg and rein aids while using half-halts to prepare for the transition to walk. Do not lengthen the reins in the walk because your horse needs a certain degree of "positive tension" in order to ride a prompt transition back to canter. There should be three to five steps of walk. When the simple change is supposed to occur at a certain point, at X for example, then the middle step of the walk should occur exactly at X. Keep your new outside rein steady and make your horse "soft" on the new inside rein. The moment in which your horse becomes light on the inside rein is the moment to ask for the transition to canter. Push your inside hip forward and give with the inside hand. Use your outside leg in the "guarding" position so that you do not accidentally push the horse's hindquarters sideways off the centerline.

Half-Volte Left, Half-Volte Right

Where You Go

In principle, this exercise is simply a more advanced version of Exercise 38 (see p. 105). The half-voltes are the same but occur with less time to "package" and prepare the horse in between them. In the previous exercise you had time on the centerline to rebalance and reestablish the connection from back to front, and give enough half-halts to bring the horse's weight back onto his haunches, whereas in this exercise, the change of direction must occur as instantaneously as possible. Trot around the track to the left. At a point of your choice—we're using B in this example—ride a half-volte ending on the centerline at X. Immediately afterward ride a half volte to the right.

Why You Do It

This exercise shows whether the horse can change the bend from one direction to the other completely, smoothly, and fluidly without loosing impulsion or rhythm.

Here's How

1 Trot around the arena on the left rein. As you turn off the track at B, beginning your half-volte, keep your eyes focused on the centerline (X), using A and C as reference points if necessary. (Note: You can also place two cones to the left and right of X for visual assistance).

2 Ride the half-volte as you did in Step 2 in Exercise 38 (see p. 105). As you come onto the centerline, "enclose" the horse with aids from both your legs and both reins. Use the right rein to straighten the horse's neck. The horse should be straight with all four feet on the center-

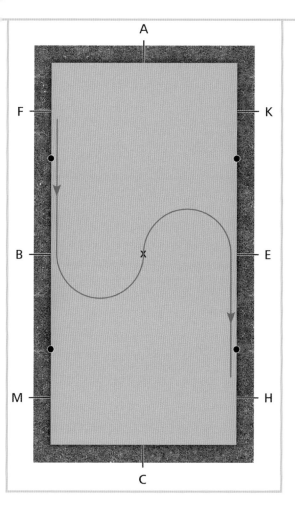

A

F ——— K

B ——— x ——— E

M ——— H

C

5 As you come back onto the track, straighten the horse again, and ride actively forward to reestablish any impulsion that may have been lost during the voltes.

6 Repeat the exercise, starting on the right rein.

7 This exercise can also be ridden in canter if the horse and rider have sufficient skill and experience. Ride a simple change in the middle point between the half-voltes (in this example, at X) to change leads, with three to five steps of walk along the centerline.

Having Problems?

- *Your horse tends to "fall out" through his outside shoulder, especially as you approach the track during the second half-volte, and you reach the track too early.* You must analyze the way in which you use your outside rein. Is your horse's neck coming straight out of his shoulders, or have you pulled his whole head and neck to the inside with your inside rein? In this case, less bend is more! When the horse is correctly bent to the inside, you should only see the side of his inside eye and the edge of his inside nostril. Increase the use of your weight aids and diminish the rein aids you use to steer your horse through the volte. In this case I might also decide to steer my horse to turn just inside the track so he must accept my outside aids and isn't simply reacting to the presence of the wall or fence. I will straighten the horse on this inside track (also known as the second track) and then return to the outside track. It is often the case that riders "fall asleep" in the second half-volte because the approaching track points the horse more or less in the right direction. However, you will find your horse

line for an instant before turning into and completing the second half-volte.

3 In the next moment, shift your weight to the right (now your inside), adjust your legs appropriately (right leg at the girth and left leg in the "guarding" position behind the girth) and your reins so that you can bend the horse right for the second volte.

4 Look toward the point at which you should reach the track—in this case, E. Make sure the horse is sufficiently bent by using your right rein and both your legs. Do not allow the horse to overbend his neck to the inside of the volte while "falling out" through his outside (left) shoulder.

happily recognizes this kind of lack of direction and begins to make the half-volte less and less round until you nearly have to ride a corner to return onto the track. So, be strict about accuracy—with yourself and your horse!

- *Your horse resists flexing and bending laterally, especially in the second half-volte.* This occurs when the horse is not yet supple enough to change the lateral bend as quickly as this exercise requires. The horse reacts to the rider's attempts to change the bend by tightening his body, and the tension then carries over into the second half-volte. To correct this, continue to ride straight ahead on the centerline for a few extra steps following the first half-volte, until your horse accepts the new inside rein without resistance. Only then ride into the second half-volte, making sure to use both legs, as well as the reins, to ask him to bend. Your inside leg should almost "push" the horse's rib cage to the outside while your outside leg "pushes" the horse's hindquarters slightly to the inside. This will enable the horse's hind hooves to follow along the path made by his front hooves. As the horse moves his rib cage over, his neck softens to the inside, and his inside hip lowers so he automatically steps farther underneath his center of gravity with his inside hind leg. *Voila,* the horse is laterally bent! You can also correct this problem by riding a transition to walk in the half-volte, working on the bend in the walk, and then picking up trot again only when the bend has been obtained. Do not ignore the problem if your horse refuses to bend, as this issue often leads to other problems, such as rushing.

Walk-Trot Voltes

Where You Go

Ride along the track in trot on the left rein. At A (for example), ride a volte from the track of a diameter of your choosing (6, 8, or 10 meters—starting with larger voltes). During the volte, ask for a downward transition to walk, allow the horse to take a few steps, and then transition back up to trot to finish the volte and continue around the arena. Repeat the exercise at B, and at other points in the arena, until you have ridden many in each direction. Gradually decrease the size of the voltes that you ride.

Why You Do It

This exercise improves the horse's lateral bend, ability to collect, and overall "throughness."

Here's How

1 As depicted in the diagram, trot along the track on the left rein. After a preparatory half-halt, ride a 10-meter volte at A.

2 Shorten the horse's stride before and during the volte with frequent half-halts until the horse is in collected trot.

3 Ride approximately one-third of the way around the volte and transition to walk. Try to use mostly your seat to ride the downward transition so your hands can keep the horse soft and happy in the contact. *Do not* pull on or constantly "hold" with the reins during the entire downward transition! This will not allow the horse to move over his back, and the beneficial effects of the transition will be lost.

4 As soon as the horse begins to walk, give with the inside (left) rein so the horse remains content in the contact and so the

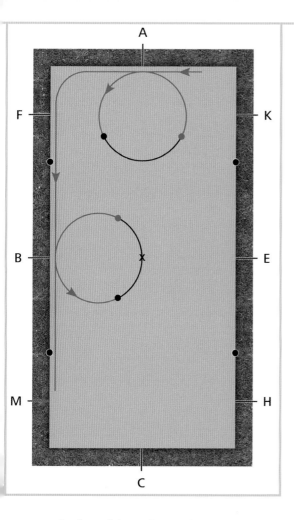

like aid for the trot transition. Give with the inside (left) hand and sit with the horse's movement.

6 After completing the volte at A, trot along the rail to B and repeat the exercise. Do more voltes around the arena in both directions. Gradually decrease the size of the volte, and reduce the number of walk steps you allow between transitions to two or three steps at the most. When your horse is sufficiently on the aids, you can even try to ride more than one walk-trot transition within each volte.

7 Make sure the transitions in the voltes are mistake-free and obtained using subtle aids while still occurring promptly! After your horse has successfully completed the exercise several times, he should be allowed to stretch forward and downward.

The Benefits of Transitions
While transitions are basic work, they should not be overlooked since such simple exercises have a fantastically positive influence on the horse and provide multiple benefits. Transitions between trot and canter, for example, have a loosening and suppling effect on the horse, while transitions to and from the walk have a collecting effect. Transitions *within* the trot and canter (changes of pace) encourage the horse's hind legs to reach farther under his body, thereby improving the "roundness" and expression of the gait. In transitions, the rider uses half-halts to direct the dynamic energy created by the driving aids to the horse's hindquarters. The rein aids are used only in moderation.

rhythm of the gait remains pure. Do not, however, lengthen the reins because you must transition to trot almost immediately, and the horse needs to "stay together" to do that. Maintaining contact and a soft connection means you can expect a more energetic and punctual upward transition to trot than you would if you had given the horse a break and let the reins go long.

5 After only a few steps of walk and while still in the second third of the volte, half-halt to get the horse's attention and ride the transition back to trot. Your legs, which during the walk had "breathed" with the horse as they lay softly against his sides, should give a quick, impulse-

Trot Volte to Halt

Where You Go

Ride in trot on the left rein along the track. Just before B, ride a volte (still in trot). Use the volte to send your horse's hind legs farther under his body and to achieve a more uphill balance. Upon returning to the track, transition to halt directly after the volte—you should be on the rail at B when you halt. After the halt, return to trot on the long side.

Why You Do It

This exercise corrects problems in the transition to the halt. Many horses start to rush or "run away" when they realize a transition to halt is approaching: They stiffen their muscles, their strides become quicker, and they may completely ignore the rider's collecting aids, which leads to problems in the rein contact. Some horses start to pull against the rider's hands and become heavy on their forehands, while others brace with the muscles under their necks and come "above the bit." By riding a volte just before the halt, the rider can keep the horse more supple at the poll, which benefits the rein contact, and she is also able to better regulate the horse's speed and tempo.

This exercise also helps correct horses that consistently halt with one hind leg trailing out behind them. For example, if your horse tends to halt with his left hind leg out behind, ride a volte to the left before the halt, activating the left (inside) hind leg so that it steps farther under the horse's body. This will help lead to a square halt. Uneven muscling of the hindquarters is often the reason that a horse halts with one hind leg trailing. Use this exercise to focus on the horse's weaker side so the weaker hind leg is encouraged to step farther forward under the horse's body.

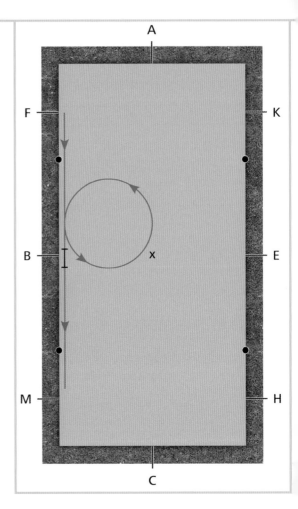

Here's How

1 Ride along the rail at a trot on the left rein. On the long side, just before B, half-halt and begin a volte. Use both legs (in the appropriate position) to send the horse forward into a briefly holding rein. After this aid, be passive again so that the horse does not become tense. In principle you can alternate giving an aid with being passive in the rhythm of the movement: one step, half-halt; the next step, relax the hands and seat without giving an aid; the next step, half-halt; and so on.

Here, a square halt is achieved after using Exercise 41 to correct Isidor's tendency to stop with one hind leg trailing out behind.

2 As you return to the track, straighten the horse while maintaining the same rhythm of half-halts. After a moment of "giving" (relaxing hands and seat), give the aid for the full halt. This aid is generally given in the same way as for a half-halt, but it is applied for a moment longer. When asking for the halt, don't sit too heavily in the saddle or you will push your horse's back down. Instead, push your pelvis toward the pommel of your saddle while sitting on the front edge of your seat bones. Do not sit on your entire seat. Your calves should gently enclose the horse while your thighs hang down without tensing or gripping.

3 Once your horse comes to a halt, soften your hands so the horse can bring his nose slightly forward. When you hold the contact too tightly in this moment, the horse is likely to step backward. Sit with enough "positive tension" in your body to tell the horse to remain standing square and immobile. If you are lucky the horse may come to a halt even when you collapse and slump due to a lack of "positive tension," but the horse definitely *will not* perform a prompt transition back to trot this way—and that is the next required movement!

4 Gain your horse's attention by momentarily increasing the pressure of your seat bones, pushing forward as your hands slightly close on the reins. Then release the aid for a brief moment, and ask for an upward transition to trot. Both calves should give a forward-driving aid, the left (inside) rein should soften to allow the horse to move forward while the right (outside) rein remains steady to maintain connection in the horse from back to front. Sit almost imperceptibly forward with the horse's movement. This allows him to raise his back, which is not only desirable but also necessary if he is to move off to trot with sufficient energy.

Trot Volte with Cavalletto

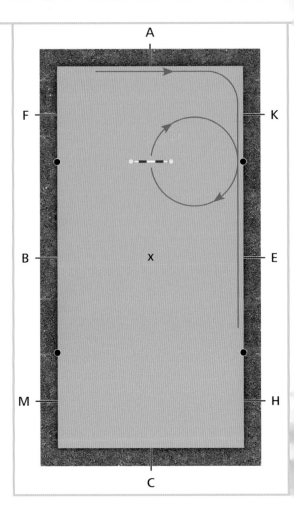

Where You Go

To prepare for this exercise, place a cavalletto on the centerline directly across from a circle point (see diagram). The cavalletto should be set on either the lowest or the middle height. Ride around the track to the right in trot. At the circle point across from the cavalletto, ride a 10-meter volte and trot over the cavalletto. Repeat the exercise in both directions.

Why You Do It

This exercise not only adds variety to standard dressage work, it also helps strengthen the muscles in the horse's hindquarters, helping to create more expression in the trot. The exercise also trains the horse to be willing and straight over cavalletti on a bending line.

Here's How

1   Trot along the track on the right rein, and ride several "normal" voltes (voltes without the cavalletto) to prepare your horse for the exercise (obtaining the necessary lateral bend, for example).

2   After riding a few preparatory voltes, continue along the rail until you reach the circle point across from the cavalletto you placed on the centerline. Begin a 10-meter volte at the point even with the cavalletto.

3   Fix your gaze on the middle of the cavalletto as you come around the curved path of the volte. Keep your horse straight between your leg and rein aids—and don't forget that your left (outside) leg should be positioned *behind* the girth! Use frequent half-halts

to keep the horse light in the hand.

4   As you approach the cavalletto, soften both hands forward to allow the horse to stretch his neck slightly forward. *Do not* drop the contact, however. Assume a slight forward seat, lightening your seat in the saddle. As you trot over the cavalletto, you should already be looking ahead at where you'll rejoin the track to keep your body correctly positioned along the curve of the volte.

5   Immediately after the cavalletto, sit more deeply in the saddle. Use a steady left (outside) rein to make sure your horse does not "fall out" along the curve. Use brief half-halts on the right (inside) rein, which should be slightly

shorter than the left rein, to guide the horse around the remaining section of the volte. Use both legs to encourage the horse's hind legs to reach forward under his body.

6 This exercise is physically challenging for the horse. In the interest of protecting his legs, the exercise should not be ridden more than four or five times in a row in each direction.

Turn-on-the-Haunches

The turn-on-the-haunches is an exercise that helps prepare the horse for collection. It is done from a walk, and the horse is prepared with half-halts to shorten the steps prior to the movement. The horse is slightly bent toward the direction he is turning, and his forehand moves in a 180-degree turn around his hindquarters, which remain almost stationary. The horse's outside foreleg (outside the bend) crosses over the inside foreleg. The hind legs do not cross: The outside hind leg steps in as small a half-circle as possible around the inside hind. The four-beat walk rhythm must be maintained during the turn-on-the-haunches.

Adele and I execute a turn-on-the-haunches.

Turn-on-the-Haunches on a Square

Where You Go

To prepare for this exercise arrange four traffic cones in the arena to mark out the corners of a square. Aligning the cones with the circle points near F and K and at B and E, as depicted in the diagram, is one option. Ride in walk around the track on the left rein. From the long side, turn off the track at B to ride around the square. Beginning at the corner of the square across from E, ride a quarter-turn-on-the-haunches (90-degree turn) to the left, walk straight to the next cone, and repeat the quarter-turn-on-the-haunches. Repeat the square several times in each direction.

Why You Do It

This exercise teaches horse and rider to begin the turn-on-the-haunches at an exact point without the support of the arena wall or fence. The horse and rider still learning this movement will benefit from executing repeated shortened versions of the turn-on-the-haunches until the horse's reaction and the rider's aids become certain enough to ride a 180-degree turn on the haunches correctly. The walk steps in between quarter-turns allow the horse to reestablish forward motion and reduce the occurrence of common mistakes in the turn, such as "sticking" and stepping backward.

Here's How

1 Walk on the left rein along the long side of the arena and turn off the track at B, riding straight across the side of the "square" toward E.

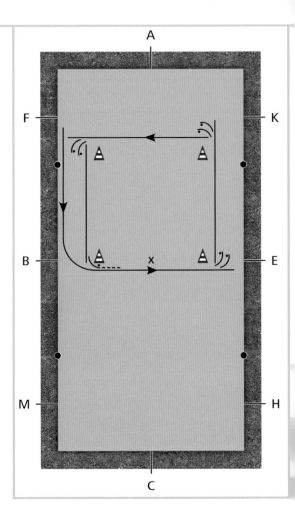

2 When you reach the cone at the corner of the square across from E, shorten your horse's walk stride with a half-halt.

3 Increase the weight on your left (inside) seat bone and flex your horse to the left. Begin the turn-on-the-haunches just as your horse passes the cone.

4 Use your left (inside) leg at the girth to keep the horse stepping actively in the four-beat walk rhythm. Keep your right (outside) leg back behind the girth. The right leg should not be used to drive the horse forward in the turn-on-the-haunches because its use will cause the horse to cross his hind legs. The exception to this rule is if the horse swings his hindquarters out and "turns around his

barrel." Then the rider's passive right "guarding" leg should assume an active function to prevent such a mistake.

5 The left rein guides the horse somewhat sideways to the left around the turn.

6 The right rein limits the amount of flexion and lateral bend but should not be held so firmly that it prevents the horse from crossing his front legs.

7 It is a common mistake to ride the turn-on-the-haunches with too much inside flexion. To prevent this mistake I recommend riding the turn in the following way: As the horse takes the first step to the left of the initial straight line, soften the left (inside) rein for the duration of one step, and in this moment, increase the feel of the right (outside) rein. This prevents the horse from over-flexing to the inside, as well as from moving too far forward. In the next step, use the left rein to guide the horse sideways around the turn, slightly softening the right rein at the moment to allow for this.

8 Once you have completed the 90-degree turn-on-the-haunches, use your left leg and right rein to prevent the horse from continuing to turn. Weight both seat bones evenly and adjust your leg position to send the horse straight forward.

9 At the next cone, begin another 90-degree turn-on-the-haunches. Repeat on all four sides of the square.

10 Practice in the other direction as well. Try it by adding a transition to halt both before and after the turn-on-the-haunches.

Having Problems?

- *Your horse is reluctant in the turn-on-the-haunches*. Does your horse "stick" and pivot on one or both hind legs? Or maybe he steps backward? To correct these mistakes, ride several turns with clearly increased forward movement, even if the turn-on-the-haunches becomes way too large in the process. The basic elements of the movement must function before the details can be perfected. Don't fall prey to pushing the horse around the turn with your outside leg. The horse will not turn correctly this way. Make the whole turn-on-the-haunches larger so that the hind hooves step around a larger half-circle.

- *Your horse hurries around the turn*. Slow the tempo by using your inside leg and outside rein. Take your time, ride one step at a time, and do not let the horse take control and turn by himself! Maintain your own control over every single step, as well as the flexion and bend!

- *Problems arise in the rein contact as you prepare to make the turn-on-the-haunches*. Perhaps your horse becomes strong in the hand and refuses to accept your aids for flexion to the inside. As a rule, only begin turn-on-the-haunches exercises when the horse is supple, soft at the poll, and well in hand. To better prepare the horse for the movement, approach the turn in shoulder-in.

Turn-on-the-Haunches on the Centerline with Cavalletti

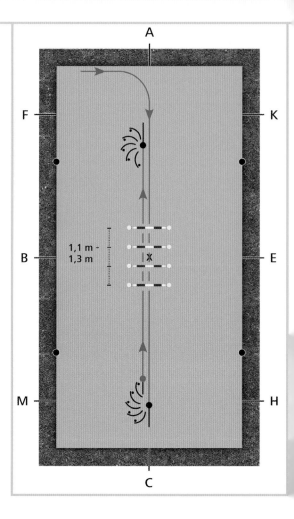

Where You Go

Only attempt this exercise when your horse is familiar with cavalletti and has previously schooled turn-on-the-haunches. If attempted before the horse is ready, the exercise will not go well and the trusting relationship between horse and rider could be damaged. To prepare for this exercise, place three to four cavalletti at X on the centerline. Set the distances between the cavalletti to fit your horse's normal or even slightly shortened trot stride (about 3.5 to 4.25 feet or 1.1 to 1.3 meters). Ride in working trot along the track on the right rein. Turn up the centerline at A and ride over the cavalletti at X. As you ride over the cavalletti, allow the horse to trot more forward. After the cavalletti, collect the trot. With enough room before the end of the centerline, ride a transition to walk between M and H, and immediately ride a turn-on-the-haunches to the right. After the turn, pick up the trot again, and trot back over the cavalletti at X. As you ride over the cavalletti, allow the horse to trot more forward. After the cavalletti, collect the trot again. Ride a transition to walk between F and K, and do a turn-on-the-haunches to the left to complete the exercise.

Why You Do It

This exercise teaches the horse to flexibly change from a stretching frame to the uphill balance required for initial collected movements. This is an important element in the horse's training and ultimately improves "throughness." The rider must be able to alternate between the dressage seat and the forward seat over the cavalletti, and she must be able to quickly and effectively rebalance the horse in order to ride the turn-on-the-haunches at each end of the centerline.

Here's how

1 Begin by tracking right in trot, and turn up the centerline at A. Get your horse's attention before the cavalletti at X with half-halts. Right before the cavalletti, slightly lighten your seat to free the horse's back, and allow the horse to stretch forward-and-downward by soft-

ening your hands toward his mouth.

2 Stay with your horse's movement as his impulsion and elevation increases over the cavalletti.

3 After the cavalletti, sit deeply in the saddle again, and collect the horse's increased impulsion with an elastic hand. The goal is to *decrease* the ground cover of the horse's trot stride while *maintaining* the cadence and *increasing* elevation. Remember to truly "give" after every half-halt so that the next half-halt can be effective.

4 With enough room before the short side—between M and H—transition to walk. As you ride the transition you should already be preparing for the turn-on-the-haunches to the right by shifting your weight appropriately and acquiring right flexion.

5 Ride one stride straight ahead in walk, and then immediately begin the turn-on-the-haunches to the right (see aids in Exercise 43, p. 114). Use only your right leg to drive the horse forward and the right rein to guide the horse's forehand around the turn. The left rein ensures the horse does not over-bend to the right. Your left leg should come into play if the horse's hindquarters start to swing out to the left.

6 When the horse has turned 180 degrees and is facing in the opposite direction, down the centerline toward A, straighten him, ride one stride in walk and then pick up the trot.

7 Build up controlled forward energy on the approach to the cavalletti. Note: This *does not* mean rush the horse over the poles!

8 Continue as described in Steps 1 through 5, but ride the next turn-on-the-haunches to the left.

9 Only repeat the exercise a few times in a row, as it is tiring for the horse.

10 You can modify the exercise by riding a halt before each turn-on-the-haunches. After the turn, halt again, and then pick up the trot directly out of the halt.

Isidor and I complete a turn-on-the-haunches to the right as I look toward the centerline.

Incorporating
Lateral Movements

Once you have schooled your horse using the earlier exercises in this book, including many transitions and straightening exercises so he reliably steps energetically underneath himself with his hind legs, it is time to add more lateral movements to your training. In shoulder-in, haunches-in, and half-pass the horse is flexed and laterally bent, and the haunches move on a different track than the forehand. There is always a risk that the horse will lose the rhythm while moving forward-and-sideways in these lateral movements, which is why a certain degree of collection is a prerequisite. However, schooling these lateral movements also improves the horse's ability to collect. Generally in dressage competition, lateral movements are shown in trot and canter, but the walk provides more time for horse and rider to become accustomed to the exercises.

Shoulder-Fore, Shoulder-In, Haunches-In, and Haunches-Out

Shoulder-in is generally the first lateral movement involving collection to be taught to the horse. Shoulder-fore serves as preparation for shoulder-in, or can be used as an easier form of the movement. In shoulder-fore, the horse is flexed and laterally bent only slightly, with his hindquarters on one track and his forehand positioned to the inside. The result is the horse moves with his body at less of an angle to the path of travel than the shoulder-in (see below). The horse's inside hind leg steps in between the hoofprints made by the front feet. His

Shoulder-fore in canter.

Shoulder-in in trot. Adele's outside foreleg exactly covers her inside hind leg.

inside, away from the direction of travel (which remains straight ahead), and his forehand is brought to the inside of the track. When the horse is viewed from the front, the horse's outside foreleg covers his inside hind leg (it should be directly in front of the hind leg) as the horse moves on "three tracks." The inside legs cross in front of the outside legs. Note: The horse should not be positioned at more than a 30-degree angle to the track on which the hindquarters are traveling.

Shoulder-in increases the horse's "thoroughness" by improving lateral bend and thereby straightness. The horse becomes more supple at the poll, and over time he will move more freely out of the shoulder. Because of the angle of travel, the horse's inside hind leg becomes accustomed to carrying more weight. The rider can better influence the horse's inside hind leg with the inside leg aid because the angle prevents the horse from evading as the rider's inside leg is applied. This improves the horse's reaction to the leg aids.

Haunches-in (travers) is more challenging for the horse than shoulder-in because he must move in the same direction he is bent. In this movement, his forehand remains on the track while his hindquarters are positioned toward the inside. As mentioned, the horse is flexed and bent laterally in the direction of travel, around the rider's inside leg. When viewed from in front or behind, the horse moves on "four tracks," with all four legs visible.

Even though the exercises that follow do not incorporate it, I should mention *haunches-out* (renvers). Haunches-out is the inverse of haunches-in: The horse's forehand comes to the inside of the track while the haunches remain on the track. As with the haunches-in, the horse is flexed and bent in the direction of travel.

outside shoulder is positioned more or less in line with his inside hip. It is very important to maintain the rhythm and forward motion of the horse's gait when schooling shoulder-fore.

As mentioned, shoulder-in is really just shoulder-fore with increased angle. The horse is flexed and laterally bent to the

Haunches-in to the left, viewed from the front...   and from behind.

Volte–Shoulder-In, Volte–Shoulder-In

Where You Go

Ride in collected trot, tracking right through the short side of the arena by A. In the second corner of the short side, ride an 10-meter volte. Upon exiting the volte, ride directly into shoulder-in on the long side. Maintain the same flexion and lateral bend in the shoulder-in that you achieved in the volte. After a few steps of shoulder-in, ride another volte at E. Again, exit the volte in shoulder-in on the track. End the shoulder-in at H by bringing the horse's forehand back onto the track and straightening the horse before rounding the corner onto the short side.

Why You Do It

The voltes in this exercise help position the horse for the shoulder-in. This makes it an especially beneficial one for horses that are not very experienced with shoulder-in. The short stretches of shoulder-in are a "friendly" introduction for the inexperienced horse or rider. Just as the horse may begin to waver in the angle of the shoulder-in, the rider can turn onto another volte and reestablish the correct flexion and lateral bend.

Here's How

1 Begin in collected trot on the right rein. As you pass A on the short side of the arena, prepare to ride a volte, and begin an 10-meter volte in the second corner.

2 Exit the volte on the long side at K and ride right into shoulder-in. Maintain the flexion and bend that you achieved in the volte—ride almost as if you are about

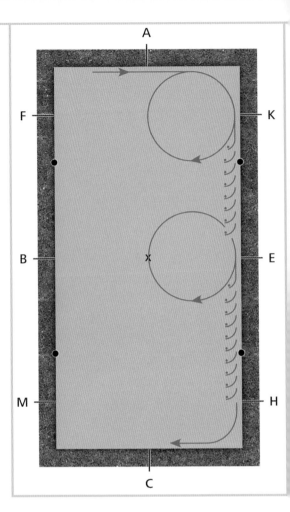

to ride onto another volte. Weight your inside (right) seat bone more than the outside (left), but not so much as to push the horse's hindquarters to the outside. Your inside leg is positioned at the girth and maintains the horse's forward movement as well as the bend through his rib cage. Your outside leg stays back behind the girth, as it was in the volte, and helps keep the bend and the forward movement, while also preventing the haunches from swinging out. (It is not uncommon to hear a horse's hind feet hitting the wall in an indoor arena if his hind end swings out during shoulder-in!) The inside rein should be slightly shortened. It is responsible for the inside flexion and guides the horse's forehand off the track. Once the horse is positioned in the correct angle in the shoulder-in, the inside rein can be repeatedly momentarily softened—this also tests the horse's balance and self-carriage. The outside rein controls the degree to which the horse's neck comes to the inside and acts like a barrier for the horse's outside shoulder, since that shoulder is no longer on the track against the wall or fence.

3 At E on the long side, ride into another 10-meter volte while maintaining the horse's bend from nose to tail. Increase the use of your outside seat bone to keep the horse's hindquarters straight behind his forehand on the volte. If needed, ride with increased energy on the volte. Up until the moment you turn onto the volte, keep a steady contact with the outside rein so the horse does not "fall onto" his inside shoulder. It is important to keep the horse's inside shoulder "free" in the shoulder-in so that the inside foreleg can cross properly over the outside foreleg as you proceed down the rail.

4 As you ride out of the second volte, ride seamlessly into the next shoulder-in. You may need the use of both reins briefly to prevent the horse from "wandering" toward the inside with his whole body and his haunches leaving the track.

5 To end the shoulder-in at H, use the outside rein to guide the horse's forehand back onto the track. Weight both seat bones evenly and use equal pressure from both calves at the girth to tell the horse to move on straight ahead.

6 Ride the exercise in both directions.

7 The more experienced horse and rider can try this exercise on the centerline, with one or two voltes, depending on the size of the arena.

I establish flexion and lateral bend in a volte to the right.

Having Problems?

- *Your horse over-bends his neck to the inside and leaves his forelegs on the track.* You are likely trying to ride the shoulder-in just with the inside rein. Straighten the horse and put him more on the outside rein. Ride on a bending line and practice bending the horse while repeatedly "giving" on the inside rein—all without the horse changing his positioning. Once this goes well, try the shoulder-in again. Do not forget to keep a steady contact with your outside rein!

- *Your horse brings his forehand too far to the inside. You are pushing the haunches out instead of bringing the shoulders in*—or riding a leg-yield! The leg-yield has more angle than the shoulder-in and has flexion, but it doesn't have lateral bend. Leg-yield is a suppling exercise but not a collecting exercise (see more about using leg-yield in schooling exercises on p. 64). This mistake begins with overuse of the inside rein, then often the rider tries to correct this with increased use of her inside leg, usually drawing it back in a misguided effort to increase its effect (the classic positioning of the forward-sideways driving leg aid in the leg-yield). Instead, increase the use of your outside rein to bring the horse's shoulders closer to the track. Use your outside leg to prevent the haunches from "falling out." It is helpful to ride this exercise in walk while correcting this problem.

Volte–Shoulder-In, Volte–Haunches-In

Where You Go

Begin in collected trot and when you reach the second corner of the short side by A, ride a 10-meter volte. After the volte, ride directly into *shoulder-in* at K on the long side. At the middle of the long side (E), ride onto a second volte the same size as the first. After this volte, ride directly into haunches-in on the long side. End *haunches-in* at H, before the end of the long side.

Why You Do It

Combining these two lateral movements with voltes improves the rider's coordination and her ability to administer the aids. The horse will gain suppleness and work toward greater flexibility in the shoulders and hind end. The voltes help prepare the horse for the two lateral movements: The *beginning* of the volte (the curved path you travel as you leave the track and start the volte) requires the same bend and balance as the shoulder-in, while the end of the volte (the curved path you travel as you leave the volte and come back to the track) is the same positioning as the haunches-in.

Here's How

1 Begin the exercise the same as Exercise 45 (p. 122), riding a 10-meter volte in collected trot in the second corner of the short side by A, and then carrying over the same degree of bend and same position into the shoulder-in on the long side.

2 At E in the middle of the long side, ride out of the shoulder-in onto a second 8-meter volte.

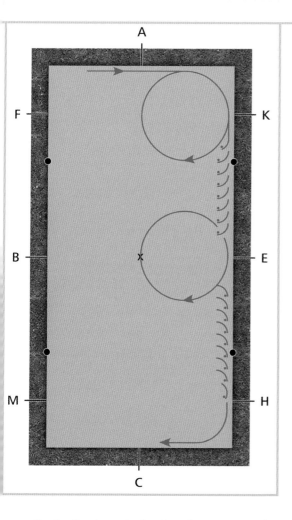

3 As the horse's forehand returns to the track after the volte, do not bring the haunches back onto the track, but rather keep the positioning from the last step of the volte and just continue it on down the long side. Keep your weight shifted slightly more onto your inside (right) seat bone. Use your inside leg at the girth to bend the horse's body and to maintain the forward movement. Your outside (left) leg should be behind the girth to move the haunches sideways. Shorten the inside rein to maintain the flexion while the outside rein limits the flexion, as well as the angle of travel.

4 To end the haunches-in at the end of the long side, straighten the horse's neck

Adele in shoulder-in after our first volte while performing the exercise on the left rein.

Adele in haunches-in after our second volte while performing the exercise on the left rein.

with the outside rein and cease to use your sideways-driving aids.

5 It is important to actively straighten your horse at the end of the long side rather than just letting him "peter out" of the movement by himself. If you are not controlling his position, he may swing his haunches to the inside in the next corner as well, even without your asking for the haunches-in.

Shoulder-In to Haunches-In on a Circle

Where You Go
Ride in trot on a 20-meter circle in the middle of the arena on the right rein. Ride several steps of shoulder-in on the circle and then several steps of haunches-in. Continue to alternate between the two lateral movements while remaining on the circle.

Why You Do It
This exercise gymnasticizes your horse and improves his ability to collect. By alternating frequently between the two movements, the horse's ability to focus increases and he responds more quickly to the aids, which leads to a greater degree of "throughness." The exercise also improves the coordination and subtlety of the rider's aids.

Here's How
1 As you approach E on the long side in collected trot, prepare to begin a 20-meter circle in the middle of the arena.

2 As you leave the track after E, make use of the horse's inside flexion on the circle to begin riding a shoulder-in. Use the inside (right) rein to maintain the flexion and to guide the horse's forehand slightly to the inside. The outside (left) rein ensures that the horse's outside shoulder does not "fall out," returning to the path of the 20-meter circle line or past it. Note, however, that the outside rein cannot be used so strongly as to hinder the flexion and angle needed to perform the shoulder-in movement correctly. Both reins can be used to prevent the horse from coming into the circle, but

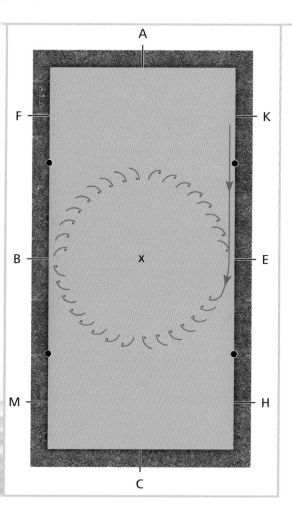

steps of correct shoulder-in with a steady degree of angle and a soft rein contact, straighten him by bringing the forehand back onto the path of the circle with the outside rein. Keep the same amount of flexion and bend.

4   In the same moment in which the forehand approaches the path of the circle, ask the horse to move his hindquarters to the inside of the circle for the haunches-in. Your outside leg behind the girth begins the haunches-in by encouraging the hind end to move to the inside of the circle. Both legs help keep the horse bent from nose to tail and moving energetically forward. As in the shoulder-in, push your inside seat bone forward. However, it can be helpful as you begin the haunches-in to push the horse's hindquarters toward the inside with your outside seat bone. Make sure to stretch your back straight up above your hips; do not lean to the outside during this movement! Use the inside rein to obtain the inside flexion. It can also have a sideways-guiding effect if needed.

5   End the haunches-in by bringing the hindquarters back onto the line of the circle. Maintain the bend in the horse's body. Keep enough connection on the outside rein to make sure your horse doesn't "fall out" through the outside shoulder. When your horse is properly on the outside rein, his shoulders remain moveable, and it should be no problem to move them to the inside directly after the haunches-in in order to start another shoulder-in.

6   This exercise can also be ridden in canter.

they must be instantly lightened once the horse comprehends the desired path of travel. In the next shoulder-in it is likely this rein aid will no longer be necessary. During the course of the exercise, the horse should become lighter and lighter on the inside rein. The rider's inside seat bone should be weighted more heavily than the outside. The inside leg drives the horse forward at the girth and the outside leg is positioned behind the girth to keep the haunches from "falling out." This is especially necessary in this exercise since there isn't a fence or wall to limit the horse and because the horse is moving on a curved line.

3   After your horse has completed a few

Spiral In, Haunches-In, Spiral Out, Shoulder-In

Where You Go

Ride in collected trot on a 20-meter circle at one end of the arena. Spiral in on the circle while riding haunches-in. Once you have spiraled in to a volte, change from haunches-in to shoulder-in. Spiral back out onto the 20-meter circle while riding shoulder-in. Once you are back on the 20-meter circle, straighten your horse and ride straight ahead down the track.

Why You Do It

Since this exercise asks the horse to move laterally on a progressively smaller circle, it encourages the horse to engage his hindquarters, and they are therefore strengthened. In this exercise the "normal" positioning of the horse is reversed: Usually, on a straight line the horse's haunches follow the shoulders, but in this case, the horse spirals in and out with his hindquarters "leading." This helps improve the rider's feel for correcting instances where the horse's shoulders or haunches "fall out," such as can happen when riding a volte. A rider that has practiced this exercise will be more quickly able to correct mistakes in the horse's straightness. In addition, the exercise tests the correct use of the outside rein.

Here's How

1 Begin in collected trot on the long side, tracking right. At A, ride a 20-meter circle. On the open side of the circle ask the horse for haunches-in: Increase the

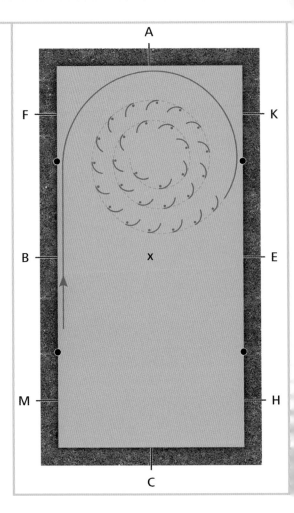

horse's inside flexion with your inside (right) rein and weight your inside seat bone more heavily. Use the inside leg at the girth to drive the horse forward and the outside (left) leg a hand's-width behind the girth to bring the haunches to the inside of the circle's path.

2 Keep a steady connection with the outside rein, but not so much as to prevent the horse from bending from nose to tail.

3 As soon as your horse is positioned in haunches-in, begin to spiral in on the circle. Use an inside opening rein to guide the horse sideways onto the next, smaller-sized circle. The outside rein can soften slightly to allow the horse

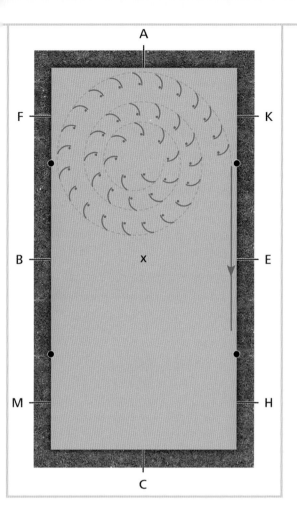

If you are unable to bring the horse's forehand to the middle of the circle, you probably have too much angle.

5 Once you have spiraled onto the smallest size circle in the center, bring the horse's haunches back onto the same track as his forehand.

6 Begin to spiral outward on the circle. Position the horse in shoulder-in as soon as you have moved onto the first larger-size circle of the spiral.

7 Use an opening inside rein to guide the horse's forehand to the inside of the circle's path. Give this aid only for brief moments, but frequently, so the horse cannot lean on the rein. The outside rein should keep a steady contact while still allowing the horse's forehand to be positioned to the inside. Your inside hip should be forward. Don't, however, overexaggerate the weight on your inside seat bone or the horse will swing his haunches out and perform a leg-yield rather than shoulder-in. Your inside leg drives at the girth and is also responsible for bending the horse laterally through his body. The outside leg is positioned behind the girth in the "guarding" position and prevents the horse from "falling out" past the desired circle size.

8 Spiral out gradually. Give the aids and then become passive briefly so the horse has time to adjust his balance to the changing circle size. This way you will also have a chance to make sure the horse is correctly positioned and carrying himself properly.

9 Once you are back on a 20-meter circle, end the exercise by straightening the horse on the long side after K and riding straight ahead.

to move inward, but it should not be "dropped," causing a loss of connection to the horse's mouth. Lost contact means a loss of necessary "positive tension" in the horse and will put him on his forehand. Do not rush to the center of the circle—spiral in gradually. Continue to put your horse on the outside rein while giving with the inside rein as you spiral inward.

4 Use your seat and leg aids to keep the horse positioned in haunches-in as he moves inward on the spiral. Note that the exercise is easier if the horse is not positioned at a steep angle in haunches-in. As horse and rider gain experience, the degree of difficulty can be increased.

Shoulder-In, Halt, Shoulder-In

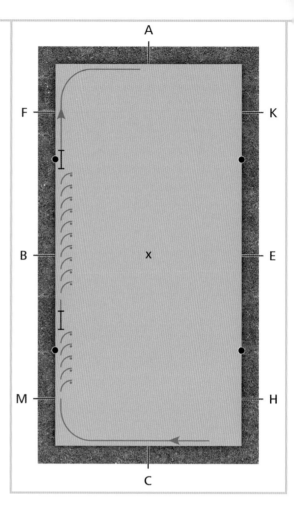

Where You Go

Ride shoulder-in in collected trot on the long side of the arena. After a number of strides, guide the horse's forehand back onto the track while riding a transition to halt. Then transition back to trot, ride a few more meters of shoulder-in, and halt again. Repeat the sequence the length of the long side.

Why You Do It

This exercise does a good job correcting horses that tend to halt with one hind leg trailing out behind them. When the *inside* hind leg is the leg that trails out behind at the halt, this exercise will encourage it to step up square. Horses that attempt to run through the aids for the halt, leading to problems in the connection from back to front, also benefit from work in shoulder-in as preparation for the halt.

Here's How

1   Ride along the short side of the arena by C in collected trot, tracking right. Trot through the second corner and onto the long side. At M, begin to ride shoulder-in. Ride shoulder-in for a number of strides, making especially sure the horse is stepping actively behind. Test whether your horse is truly on the outside (left) rein by "giving" on the inside (right) rein.

2   Guide the forehand back to the track with the outside rein once your horse demonstrates self-carriage. This can be done gradually by reducing the angle of the horse's position to the track over the course of a few steps. As you straighten the horse, ask him to step further un-derneath himself with his hind legs, and then ride a transition to halt. The halt transition should occur immediately af-ter the shoulder-in or the beneficial ef-fect of the lateral movement will be lost. It is also important that you apply your outside leg in the halt transition to pre-vent the haunches from swinging out and the horse halting crookedly.

3   After the halt, return to the trot, and ride shoulder-in again in preparation for another halt further down the long side. As your horse becomes familiar with the exercise, decrease the number of steps of shoulder-in and decrease the degree of angle of the shoulder-in before the

Isidor in shoulder-in prior to a halt.

halt transition. The horse will eventually become more sensitized to your inside leg so you can increase the activity of the inside hind leg without riding a full shoulder-in.

Half-Pass

Once the horse is confirmed in shoulder-in and haunches-in, you can begin work in the half-pass. In the half-pass the horse moves with his body nearly parallel to the track and his forehand leading slightly. He should be flexed and bent in the direction of travel, with his outside legs crossing over his inside legs. Half-pass is essentially a variation of haunches-in, but one where you move along a diagonal line.

Half-pass to the left viewed from the front. My inside shoulder should be a bit farther back so I am better positioned in the direction of the horse's movement.

Half-pass to the left viewed from behind. Here you can clearly see the crossing of Adele's hind legs.

Shoulder-In, Half-Pass, Shoulder-In, Half-Pass

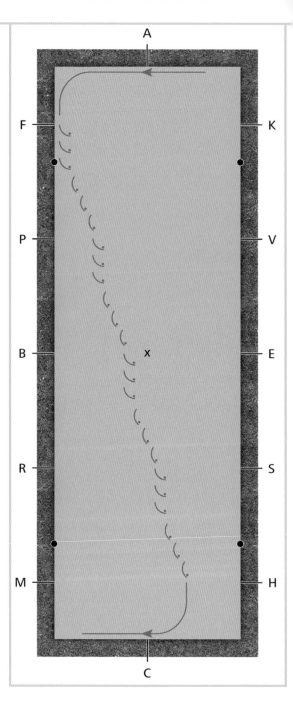

Where You Go

Ride in collected trot along the short side by A and through the second corner on the left rein. On the long side at F, begin shoulder-in. After a few steps, ride half-pass out of the shoulder-in. After a few steps of half-pass on the diagonal, return to shoulder-in on a line that is parallel to the long side. After a few more steps of shoulder-in, return to half-pass. End the half-pass by riding straight ahead for the final strides until you reach the short side. Upon reaching the short side, track right.

Why You Do It

Riding shoulder-in is ideal preparation for the half-pass since the shoulder-in establishes the correct lateral bend in the horse. If your horse begins to lose the necessary bend or impulsion while attempting the half-pass, you can cease to ride half-pass and go right back to shoulder-in, reestablishing the correct flexion, bend, and forward movement. Once your horse remains properly balanced and soft in the hand in the shoulder-in, you can attempt a few strides of half-pass. This is an effective way to nip "half-pass problems" in the bud and efficiently proceed ahead with further half-pass work.

Here's How

1 On the left rein, ride the collected trot along the short side past A and through the second corner. At F on the long side,

begin to ride shoulder-in. Increase the weight on your inside (left) seat bone, bend the horse around your inside leg, and place your outside (right) leg in the "guarding" position to prevent the haunches from "falling out." Shorten your inside rein and use it to maintain the inside flexion and bend, as well as to initially guide the horse's forehand to an inside track. Soften the inside rein as soon as the horse is positioned correctly. The outside rein maintains the connection from back to front and prevents the forehand from drifting back to the track.

2 Next, ride a half-pass out of the shoulder-in. Draw an imaginary diagonal line from your horse to a point across the arena, and keep your eyes fixed on this point! You will ride your horse along this imaginary diagonal line. To begin the movement, use the inside rein more firmly, and even use an opening inside rein to help guide the horse sideways if needed. Use the outside leg to move the horse diagonally, but be careful not to press so hard with the leg that the horse leads with his haunches, losing the key positioning that was achieved by preparing for the movement in shoulder-in.

3 Be strict about keeping your horse on the imaginary diagonal line. This will help ensure that each step of the half-pass is even.

4 After several steps of half-pass, return to shoulder-in—as you cross the centerline, for example. For the transition to shoulder-in, the aids change only subtly. The outside rein stops the horse from continuing on the diagonal line and steers him straight ahead on the centerline (or another line parallel to the track). The inside rein ensures the horse maintains the correct inside bend and softens once the bend is achieved. During the half-pass the rider's seat bones swing forward-and-sideways, whereas in the shoulder-in they swing more forward. The use of the outside leg must be adjusted appropriately so that the horse's haunches are not pushed too far inward.

5 Once the horse is trotting fluidly in shoulder-in, begin another segment of half-pass, as described in Step 2.

6 To end the exercise, straighten the horse and trot straight ahead with good impulsion toward the short side of the arena. Upon reaching the short side, track right and ride the exercise again in the new direction.

Try Walking

Don't forget that it can be very helpful to try new exercises in walk first, then in a slow trot, gradually increasing the impulsion as horse and rider gain confidence in the movement. If problems occur in the exercise—for example, if the horse loses flexion or lateral bend, or if he truly does not want to cross his legs over—ride a transition to walk and proceed with the exercise in walk. This way your aids will be more effective and you will be able to correct the horse!

Volte, Half-Pass, Volte, Half-Pass

Where You Go

Ride on the left rein in collected trot. In the second corner of the short side by A, ride a volte. As you come out of the volte at F, ride directly into a half-pass. Half-pass until you are almost to the centerline and even with P and V. Ride another volte. After the volte return to the half-pass. End the exercise by straightening the horse, riding to the opposite short side of the arena. There change direction.

Why You Do It

Like Exercise 50, this is another exercise that helps the rider prepare for the half-pass by attaining the necessary lateral bend in the volte. The exercise tests whether the horse can move from the bending line of the volte into the lateral movement, and vice versa, without losing rhythm and impulsion. If the quality of the horse's movement diminishes during the half-pass, the rider can correct this on the second volte by asking the horse to step farther underneath his body with his hind legs, as well as to increase flexion and bend, if needed.

Here's How

1. Begin at a collected trot, tracking left along the short side by A. In the second corner, ride a volte, using it to prepare for the half-pass by creating the appropriate lateral bend through the horse's body. Once the horse is carrying himself, "give" the inside rein (left) without the horse changing his line of travel or carriage.
2. Horses tend to assume that they should travel straight ahead after a volte, so

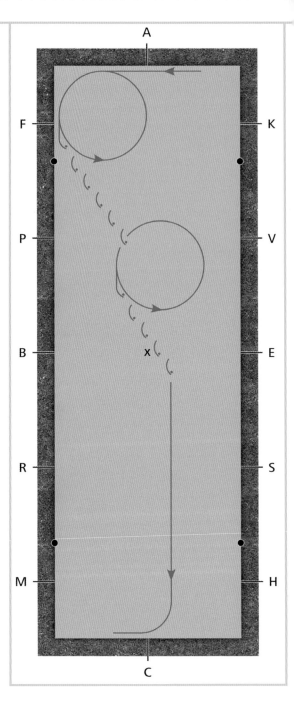

you must ride a clear transition to half-pass. Half-halt near the end of the volte to gain the horse's attention level and ensure he is sufficiently collected. Look in the direction in which you wish to go, and then keep the horse traveling along this imaginary diagonal line. Use the inside (left) rein to guide the horse's forehand sideways. Bend the horse around your inside leg while using the outside (right) leg positioned behind the girth to bring the hindquarters over. Your inside hip should be positioned forward, and the outside seat bone can also be used to transmit short, impulse-like aids to cause the horse's outside hind leg to step actively forwards-sideways. As you engage your outside aids, be careful not to use them so strongly that you "push" the hindquarters ahead of the forehand. This mistake can be easily identified and corrected with the assistance of a ground person to view the horse from the front or by looking in a mirror. If these are not available, an occasional glance over your inside shoulder will also determine whether the haunches are in the proper position. But don't forget, looking back like this can disturb the horse's balance!

3 Before riding into the second volte, shorten the horse's stride and frame while still in the half-pass. Using the outside rein, reduce the horse's sideways (diagonal) movement. Imagine that as you ride a half-halt to prepare for the volte your horse, for a brief moment, moves in place.

4 When your horse responds to this half-halt, ride onto the next volte. Be very careful with the use of your outside leg here so the horse does not perform haunches-in on the circle. If your horse has lost some of his lateral bend during the half-pass, or if he has become strung out and has begun to lean on the bit, the volte offers an excellent opportunity to correct such issues.

5 Once you have optimized the horse's balance and bend on the volte, return to the half-pass as described in Step 2. Keep your eyes fixed on the point of your next transition.

6 When you have completed several good strides of your final half-pass, straighten the horse and ride forward toward the short side with good impulsion.

The Outside Rein

It is crucial that during the half-pass the outside rein remains more or less steady. The outside rein comes less into play in the moments in which the inside rein guides the horse sideways; it has more importance in the moments in which the inside rein softens. It is then that the outside rein ensures that the amount of neck bend is limited, which is important to prevent the horse from leaning on the inside rein and eventually the inside shoulder. The latter negatively impacts the horse's ability to cross his legs over and in general causes the movement to fall apart. The outside rein also serves to "hold the horse's shoulder up" in order to free the forelegs to move expressively, as well as to keep the horse in an uphill balance with increased weight on his hind legs. After all, half-pass is a collected movement!

Half-Pass Right to X, Leg-Yield Left

Where You Go

Ride in collected trot past C on the short side, tracking right. As you ride out of the second corner onto the long side, half-pass from M away from the track toward X. Upon reaching X, change to leg-yield (see p. 64 for more). Leg-yield your horse off your right leg back to the track at F (on the same long side from which you began). Straighten your horse as you reach the track to end the exercise.

Why You Do It

The half-pass requires a higher degree of balance and collection from your horse. When horses are initially learning lateral work they are only able to show a few good strides at a time. If the rider demands that the horse perform the lateral movement beyond his current ability, the horse will gradually move less sideways, and the quality of the gait and bend will diminish until the horse ends up balancing on the rider's hand. It is not unusual to see riders attempting to salvage the half-pass with strong use of the outside leg and inside rein. This only results in the horse tilting his head (a fault) instead of bending laterally, and moving with his hind legs strung out behind him. Exercise 52 offers a solution to this problem by helping the rider reestablish connection with the outside rein and thereby keeping the horse supple at the poll and in self-carriage. As the connection improves, the horse will be able to move forward more freely.

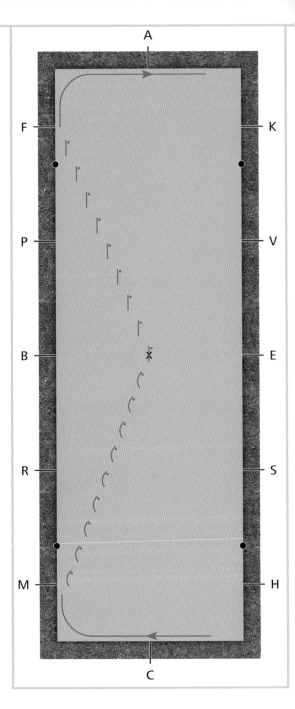

Here's How

1 Begin in collected trot on the short side of the arena by C, tracking right. As you ride out of the corner onto the long side, begin half-passing away from the

track at M. Keep your gaze fixed on X and ride toward this point.

2 During the half-pass push your inside (right) hip forward and drive with your inside leg at the girth. The rider's outside leg is positioned behind the girth and helps keep the horse's hindquarters crossing actively sideways. The horse should be flexed and bent to the right.

3 As you approach X, "flatten out" the last two steps of the half-pass so that you ride less sideways and more straight ahead. At the same time, reduce your sideways-driving seat aids and use the outside rein to limit sideways movement.

4 Cease bending your horse laterally through the body since the leg-yield requires only flexion at the poll and not bend. Begin to leg-yield your horse off the right (inside) leg. Use the left (outside) rein to guide the horse's forehand to the left. This must be done very clearly at the beginning of the leg-yield so that the horse's forehand slightly leads before the haunches. In the half-pass the haunches were moving to the left of the forehand; to switch to leg-yield, the forehand must be brought sufficiently left of the haunches. As the left rein brings the forehand to the left, the right rein remains "passive," although it is still responsible for maintaining the right flexion.

5 The rider's right leg should now slide back behind the girth to bring the horse's hindquarters to the left. The rider's right seat bone again comes into play, but this time not to bring the horse to the right but rather to push him forward-and-sideways to the left.

6 End the exercise by straightening the horse and riding for the short end. Practice the exercise in the other direction.

Half-pass to the centerline.

Half-Pass to X, Leg-Yield X to Track

Where You Go

Ride in collected trot tracking right along the short side by C. At M on the long side, begin a half-pass to the right. Half-pass until you reach X, then change to leg-yield (off the rider's left leg) and ride the rest of the diagonal (to K) in leg-yield. End the exercise by straightening the horse and trotting along the track.

Why You Do It

This exercise is helpful for horses that do not cross their legs over sufficiently in the half-pass. This is often the case with young or green horses because they simply are not yet able to collect sufficiently. The horse must be in self-carriage to be able to cross the outside fore and hind legs over the inside fore and hind legs while bending toward the direction of travel. During this exercise the horse's outside fore and hind legs *become the inside*, the flexion changes sides and the horse is no longer laterally bent after X. Leg-yield has a loosening effect upon the horse, so if the horse built up (negative) tension during the half-pass he can become relaxed and supple again in the leg-yield without avoiding crossing his legs. The exercise is also an example of dressage training using psychology: At the same point where the horse may attempt to evade, the rider asks the horse to do something easier in all respects except one crucial one (in this case, crossing the legs).

Here's How

1 Begin in collected trot on the right rein

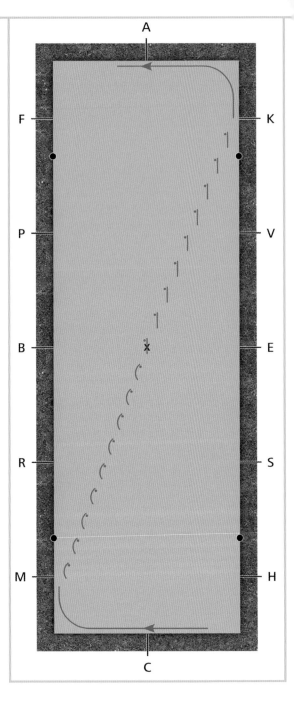

on the rail. Ride a half-pass from M on the long side to X. Keep your eyes focused on X. Your right (inside) hip is positioned forward and your right leg is at the girth to maintain the horse's lateral bend and forward movement. Your left (outside) leg stays behind the girth and encourages the horse's haunches to come sideways (on the diagonal). At the start of the half-pass use your right rein to obtain the right flexion and to guide the horse's forehand off the track. The outside rein limits the flexion and maintains the collected frame necessary for the movement.

2   When you reach X on the centerline, switch from half-pass to leg-yield. During the last few steps of the half-pass begin to straighten the horse, but don't just let the bend "peter out"—make sure you deliberately use your straightening aids. Use enough left rein to completely straighten the horse's neck so he is no longer bent and is even in both reins. Then obtain left flexion by increasing the feel on the left (now your inside) rein. At the same time redistribute the weight on your seat bones so that the left seat bone is more heavily weighted. The left leg remains behind the girth and sends the horse forward-and-sideways even more actively. Your right (now outside) leg now moves back into the "guarding" position.

3   Guide the horse's forehand sideways to the right on the diagonal with the right rein. The right rein is also responsible for keeping the forehand slightly ahead of the horse's haunches. Continuously "soften" the left rein to enable the horse's inside fore and hind legs to cross further over his outside legs.

4   Upon reaching the track at K, straighten your horse, and trot actively forward with good impulsion.

5   Practice the exercise in both directions.

Isidor and I come through the second corner on the short side—we will carry over the lateral bend, flexion, and uphill balance from the corner into the half-pass we'll begin at M.

Use the Exercise Creatively
When riding this exercise, you do not need to use the starting and ending points given in this example. You can make the half-pass steeper or shallower; you can end the half-pass and transition to leg-yield much earlier. It is not necessary to go across the entire diagonal. The exercise is most beneficial if you learn to pick the moment in the half-pass in which your horse becomes "flat," losing rhythm and impulsion, and then ride your transition to the leg-yield. Once the horse is again moving fluidly forward-and-sideways, the correction has succeeded and the exercise can end.

Half-Pass Right, Leg-Yield, Half-Pass Left

Where You Go

Track right in collected trot, beginning on the short side at C. Ride out of the second corner onto the long side, and at M, begin a half-pass right toward X. End the half-pass a few strides before the centerline, changing the flexion to the left and leg-yielding off the left leg (toward X) for a few strides. Ride a transition from leg-yield into half-pass left, back toward the track. End the exercise by straightening the horse and riding straight ahead when you reach F at the end of the long side.

Why You Do It

This exercise prepares the horse and rider for the zigzag. A seamless transition from left to right half-pass (and vice-versa) required in the zigzag is difficult for both horse and rider. It requires that the horse is confirmed in his balance, collection, suppleness, and "throughness," and that he has a quick reaction time to the aids. This exercise introduces the change of direction in the half-pass in a "user-friendly" way. The approach prevents the horse from "throwing himself" into the new direction and helps activate his new inside hind leg. The exercise is also beneficial for horses that are already familiar with the zigzag but tend to waver and make an unclear change of bend and direction.

Here's How

1 Begin in collected trot, tracking right, on the short side by C. After the second corner, begin a half-pass to the right at

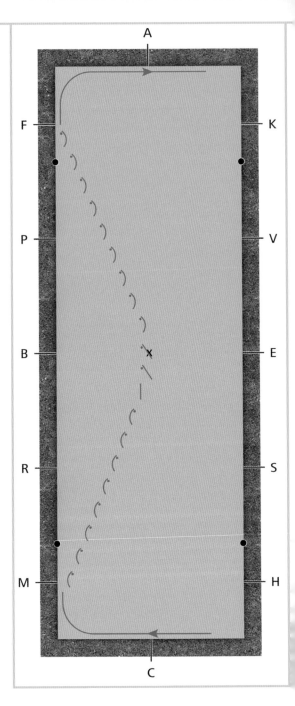

M (see Exercise 53, p. 140). Look ahead toward X.

2 End the half-pass before reaching the centerline by briefly using both seat bones weighted evenly to send the

horse straight ahead. Straighten the horse's neck with the left rein.

3 Keeping the horse parallel to the track, leg-yield off your left leg toward X. Position your left leg behind the girth to send the horse forward-and-sideways to the right. Your right leg should be in the "guarding" position. Increase the weight on your left seat bone, flex the horse left with your left rein, and limit the amount of flexion with your right rein.

4 The leg-yield need not be performed at a steep angle. After only a few steps—as soon as your horse is softly accepting the left flexion—begin half-pass to the left. Push your already weighted left seat bone more forward and stretch weight down through your left side. This will automatically bring your left leg forward to the girth where it can properly influence the horse's bend and forward movement. Initiate the half-pass by guiding the horse's forehand to the left with an opening left rein. At the same time, the right rein keeps the horse's right shoulder from "bulging out," limits the flexion left, and works together with the driving aids to keep the horse in balance. Your outside leg (which was already in the "guarding" position during the leg-yield) sends the horse's haunches to the left.

5 At first, leave enough time to change the horse's positioning between half-pass, leg-yield, and half-pass. When your horse consistently responds with good "throughness" to the aids and position changes, you can begin to ask for a more immediate response.

6 End the exercise when you reach the track at F, sending your horse straight ahead with all the aids administered equally on both sides. Ride forward with good impulsion.

Common Half-Pass Mistakes

Rhythm Issues: Mistakes in the rhythm occur when the impulsion is lost during the half-pass. As the impulsion decreases, the sideways movement also diminishes, and the rider often tries to compensate for this with increased use of the inside rein. This only causes the horse to lean on the inside rein. To solve problems with rhythm in the middle of your half-pass line, ride straight ahead for several strides or on a large curved line, reestablishing good impulsion before returning to half-pass. Often when the horse loses impulsion during the change of direction he begins the second half-pass with a nodding head—a telltale sign of a loss of rhythm. If this occurs, begin the second half-pass with less lateral bend in the horse.

Incorrect Aids: Riders are often seen using too strong an inside rein and outside leg during the half-pass. It is also common for riders not to look where they are going—it is crucial that the rider looks in the direction of travel so that her weight is distributed correctly.

Leading with the Haunches: When the horse tends to bring his haunches ahead of his forehand in the half-pass instead of correctly leading with the forehand, it is advisable to ride shoulder-in for a few steps before beginning the half-pass.

Half-Pass at All Angles

Where You Go
Starting from the long side at M, ride a half-pass to the right in trot. Vary the degree of angle of your half-pass as you go so that a few steps are more sideways and the next few steps are more forward, and so on, until you reach the track on the opposite long side. End the exercise by riding straight ahead, now on the left rein.

Why You Do It
The horse will gain suppleness and "through-ness" if you vary the degree of angle in the half-pass. He will cross his legs more clearly, and the half-pass will become more expressive. The exercise also improves the timing of the rider's aids and her feel for the degree of angle necessary to reach a certain point in the arena while riding half-pass.

Here's how
1 Begin on the right rein, passing C on the short side before asking for half-pass right at M. Ride deeply into the second corner of the short side, using the corner to obtain the flexion and lateral bend you need in the half-pass. Make sure the horse is stepping well underneath himself with his hind legs.

2 Make your first segment of half-pass more of an angle, relative to the long side. Fix your gaze on a point or letter in the first half of the arena on the opposite long side—say S. Pick a number of steps that you would like to ride for this segment of the half-pass. Then choose another letter in the second half of the arena so the degree of angle in your half-pass changes, and ride the same

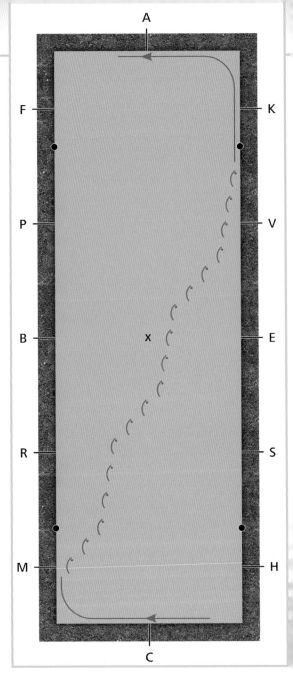

number of steps in half-pass toward it. Note there is no need to make the exercise unnecessarily difficult at the beginning, so choose an attainable number of steps for each segment of half-pass: For example, four steps toward S, four steps toward V, four steps toward E, four steps toward K. Later on you can change the pattern of the steps during the exercise

Adele in a half-pass that has significant sideways movement and is at a greater angle relative to the long side where we started the movement. In this moment, her haunches are almost leading and I should adjust my left (outside) leg to correct it.

A half-pass where we are moving more forward than sideways—at less of an angle relative to the long side.

to use varying numbers of steps, as well as varying angles of travel.

3 Aim to get an energetic response to your seat aids from the horse. Make sure to keep your horse's weight balanced on his hindquarters. Do not overly soften the left (outside) rein or the horse will shift his weight to the forehand. Be careful not to overuse your left leg—you want the horse's forehand to lead the movement, not his haunches.

4 After riding the previously determined

number of steps of toward S, begin to ride half-pass toward V. Shift your gaze to a different point of arrival on the opposite long side—one that is farther ahead of the first point.

5 Diminish your sideways-driving aids appropriately. Use your seat bones to send the horse more forward than sideways. Reduce the use of your left (outside) leg. Ride the horse forward with increased impulsion and allow a slight lengthening of his frame. These two things will be only minimally perceptible to an observer since there are only a few steps

in which you will do this and since the lateral movement inherently limits the amount of forward travel and length of frame. Nonetheless, keeping this "feeling" in mind helps prepare for the upcoming change to a half-pass that is more sideways than forward.

6 After your predetermined number of steps toward V, begin to ride your next segment. You will have advanced down the arena some so your new point of reference on the long side can be E. Send your horse's hind legs farther underneath his body and increase his degree of uphill balance so that he shortens his frame.

7 When the horse is correctly "through," this adjustment should be achieved in one stride; in the next stride the horse should already move more sideways with good cadence, picking up his legs higher than in the prior half-pass segment, and crossing them over farther. Increase your aids appropriately to accommodate this portion of the exercise.

8 Continue varying degrees of angle in the half-pass until you reach the opposite track (near K). Straighten the horse and prepare to ride the exercise in the opposite direction.

Train for the Good of the Horse
This exercise is strenuous for the horse. Allow your horse to become accustomed to its challenges gradually by sticking to short segments and increasing the number of steps in the more sideways half-pass only when the horse has had time to gain strength and conditioning. Never forget to keep your horse's fitness level in mind. Do not overface or stress your horse out of a drive for success. After all, you probably do not have to ride a double zigzag half-pass in a Grand Prix test tomorrow!

"Meaningful Training"

I would assert that all riders would vehemently dispute the belief held by some (nonriders, obviously!) that riding is nothing more than being carried around by a horse. Whether you consider yourself a competitive rider or a pleasure rider is irrelevant in this matter. Anyone that even somewhat seriously pursues this wonderful sport knows that an effort from body, mind, and spirit are necessary to form a trusting partnership with the horse, both on the ground and when working under saddle.

Along the way, evaluate the training needs of your horse. Try to determine what the horse needs to develop in terms of his musculature, and also taking into account his personality and motivation, what should be worked on and how. Be open to accepting the help of a riding instructor or a fellow rider. As the old saying goes, practice makes perfect, and with riding you must never stop learning! It is too easy for bad habits to creep in slowly and unnoticed. However, don't go to the other extreme of implementing every suggestion made by a barn mate or imitating the riding style of a competitive rider in your barn without thinking it through first.

Create your own vision for your riding and your time with your horse! Visualize a picture of a well-ridden horse with correct training, and make that vision reality by using serious information from reliable sources. Take lessons from a qualified instructor, and educate yourself by reading books, talking with successful riders, and attending clinics and seminars.

The goal of this book is to provide you with practical exercises to keep you and your horse busy for a while, and ideas for using movements and school figures in different ways. As you grow familiar with these exercises, the experience you will gain will automatically lead to new ideas and creative ways to keep your horse occupied meaningfully. There are many more possibilities here! Combine the elements provided within these pages and discover new schooling tools on your own!

Finally, I hope that this book encourages you to expand your riding horizons. Dressage can be interesting and fun for anyone, on any kind of horse. It is meaningful horse training.

Thanks

Special thanks go out to Alex and Martin for their expertise in graphic design and their work with the photos in this book. And of course to Dani, who not only had to do without me as I focused my efforts on the book but who also took the fabulous photos!

Index

Page numbers in *italics* indicate illustrations.